W9-ALF-554

ST MARTIN'S
TRUE CRIME
CLASSICS

THE JEFFREY DAHMER STORY

AN AMERICAN NIGHTMARE
(previously published as *The Milwaukee Murders*)

DON DAVIS

St. Martin's Paperbacks

The Jeffrey Dahmer Story was previously published under the title *The Milwaukee Murders.*

THE JEFFREY DAHMER STORY: AN AMERICAN NIGHTMARE

Copyright © 1991, 1992, 1995 by Don Davis.

Cover photograph by AP/Wide World Photos.

All rights reserved.

For information address St. Martin's Press, 175 Fifth Avenue, New York, NY 10010.

ISBN: 0-312-92840-8
EAN: 80312-92840-7

Printed in the United States of America

St. Martin's Paperbacks edition / November 1991
Revised St. Martin's Paperbacks edition / January 1995

St. Martin's Paperbacks are published by St. Martin's Press, 175 Fifth Avenue, New York, NY 10010.

25 24 23 22

For Russ and Randy

Acknowledgments

A book is never done by one person. The writing, research, and editing require many hands. The many people who volunteered their time and energy on this project have earned my respect and my thanks, both for their professionalism and for their efforts. They made this document better.

Special thanks to Robin, who brightens everything, even while editing a manuscript.

And to everyone at Families Against Drugs in San Diego for their friendship and support; to Ken and Sara Englade; to Herr Growald and Valerie and Jim and Tom, Mei-Mei, Mary, Linda, and Jo for putting up with me; to the dozens of good people of Ohio and Wisconsin who gave of their valuable time to share their knowledge with a stranger; to Dr. Ashok Bedi for an illuminating interview and to other experts who took time to guide me; to Mark Anderson at Marquette for his emergency assistance; to David Cornwell, for planting a seed many years ago; to my editor, Charlie Spicer, and his gang; to my agent, Mark Joly; and to Irma and Eric in Savannah, for a lifetime of encouragement.

CHAPTER ONE

Little Boy Lost

Monday, May 27, 1991

He was only fourteen years old and running for his life, trying to get away from the tall man. For a time, he thought he had made it, that he had escaped, just as his brother had done. Two young women had come out of the darkness to help him, and when the big fire engine showed up, a woman fire fighter wrapped his naked body in a blanket. Now, three policemen, shining badges and all, stood only a fingertip away as he leaned against the fender of a blue-and-white squad car.

The legs of the dark-haired, olive-skinned youngster were streaked with some of the blood that had oozed from his violated anus. Tears coated his cheeks with a dry sheen. He was cold, and his head felt stuffed with cotton because he had been drugged. Konerak Sinthasomphone was terrified, trapped in a nightmare on the hard streets of Milwaukee, still unable to do much more than shake his head and softly say, "No." But now the police were here. They would arrest the tall man, just as they had when his brother got into trouble with a man several years ago.

Monday, May 27, was a gentle night in Milwaukee as an early spring pushed away the bitter winter. A few more months, come summer, and people would flock to the streets for festivals and food and the kind of backslapping comradeship that neighborhoods in big cities enjoy. Even at this time of night, people would be sitting in the parks or coming home from the movies or just walking around two blocks over on Twenty-seventh Street. There would be plenty of people around in about a month, when the weather really warmed up. But right now, Konerak felt as alone as he ever had felt in his young life.

What he had just endured in that foul-smelling apartment with the tall man had left him confused and shattered and desperately in need of help. He knew that more bad things, things like those he had seen in the pictures scattered around the apartment, might happen if he did not get out of there.

In a stroke of good fortune, while Konerak was still passed out in the apartment the man had gone out to buy beer. The boy, in pain, awoke, managed to yank open the wooden door, and ran away.

But he could not actually run very fast because the sleeping potion had robbed him of the quickness he always showed when tearing down the sidelines on a soccer field, clipping the ball along with the side of his foot. He felt as if he were moving through heavy molasses. He told his legs to hurry, but they refused to obey his command. Instead, he sidled along in a kind of stagger; that was the best he could do. Stark terror fueled what little energy he could muster to escape, for he knew the tall man would be coming after him. Konerak could only hope someone might intervene. That was his only chance. One foot ahead of another, he wobbled along, out into the street. But the tall man was striding quickly toward him, catching up.

Konerak, a handsome Laotian youngster, had been missing from his home since the previous day, when he had vanished on his way to the usual Sunday soccer practice in Mitchell Park. As an Asian boy, he instinctively took to soccer the way American boys seem to know how to throw a baseball from the time they are in the crib. Konerak kept up with the fortunes of the Milwaukee Brewers, but they were already falling behind the pack in the American League East and it was hard to bring much enthusiasm to bear for a

3

string of losses. The Green Bay Packers were idle until fall, so football was not of interest for the time being. Soccer was where a small kid with lightning reflexes could shine. Size didn't really matter on the soccer field, and for a little guy, that was important. Konerak had dreams of becoming a professional soccer player, like his heroes Pelé, Beckenbauer, and Maradona. He religiously worked out lifting weights with his legs to make them stronger for the field and got into a game at every opportunity.

The Sinthasomphone family was relatively new to the United States. After the long, bruising conflict in Indochina was won by the Communists, the family had decided that the brutal regimes that had taken over Saigon, Phnom Penh, and Vientiane were offering only additional years of pain and hardship, despite their declarations of helping the people. In 1980, the family fled Laos, abandoning the sparkling air and the emerald mountains and lush jungles for a place that was truly foreign to them, a city in the United States, the place the American GIs who fought in Indochina used to refer to as "the World," as if Laos and Vietnam and Cambodia were on some far-distant planet. Milwaukee, which since its beginning has been a melting pot for various cultures. In Milwaukee, it is assumed that a family has roots in some foreign land and that the first generation speaks English with an accent. Their children will speak the language better, and the grandchildren will grow up with the promise and the problems of any American child. As they watch the third generation grow up, grandparents may wonder if they made the right decision in leaving the old country, as they see the kids listening to loud music and wearing their hair funny and not respecting their elders. Konerak was three years old, the youngest of eight children, when he came to Milwaukee. With the experiences he gained on the streets and in school, he was speeding up the timetable. He was Asian in heritage, but American to the core.

The flight to freedom from Laos had been arduous enough, but something else seemed to lurk about the family, something dark and unknown in the land from which freedom had beckoned. Many in the Lao community believe refugee families are not really prepared for life in an American metropolis, where the jungle is made of concrete and the predators are likely to be the most ordinary-looking people. In Indochina, in the midst of war, it was rather easy to distinguish the life-threatening situations. But in America, for the Lao, it was different. Elders say the men and women who left Laos thought they were reaching safe haven in the United States, and realized only through bitter experience that the sidewalks of America are paved not with gold, but with danger.

The Sinthasomphone family had figured that out before Konerak went missing. Three years earlier, in 1988, when Konerak's older brother was thirteen years of age, a tall blond man with strangely empty eyes had enticed the boy into his apartment, toyed with him sexually for a while, and offered to pay him fifty dollars to let the tall man take pictures of him, pictures in which the boy would not wear any clothes. The boy, frightened, dashed away and got help. Police came and arrested the tall man, and the court, in 1989, sentenced him to eight years in jail. He served ten months in a minimum-security confinement that allowed him to leave for work at night, a leash that was so loose that he occasionally returned to jail in the morning smelling of whiskey, having skipped off his job for a round of drinking. After the semi-jail time, the man was given five years of probation. The Sinthasomphone family thought the nightmare was over. They were wrong. That incident was only the prologue.

Just as his brother had made it to safety, just as in television shows he had seen where evil is always vanquished in the end, Konerak might have allowed himself in the early moments of that Monday morning to believe that he had been saved. He was away from that horrible apartment with its rancid smell, and people had reached out to help him. This was not Laos. This was America and he was an American kid. He may have thought things were turning in his favor. He was almost right.

His plight had not gone unnoticed, for extraordinarily peculiar behavior stands out even in a neighborhood that is big-city blasé about most things. Two girls from the neighborhood, Nicole Childress, eighteen, and her cousin, Sandra Smith, also eighteen, saw the disoriented boy on a darkened street, naked, with scarlet patches of blood on his behind and a dazed, uncomprehending look of fright on his young face. When they spoke to him, he could only mumble.

The girls were not passive. A tall white man came up and tried to grab the boy, but Smith would not turn him loose, holding on to an arm while her cousin ran to one of the pair of pay telephones on the corner and dialed the emergency number, 911. In minutes, Fire Engine Number 32 rolled up and the two blue-and-white squad cars of the Milwaukee Police Department arrived. Three uniformed officers stepped out.

Cops coming to such a disturbance have one thought in the front of their minds, to restore order as fast as possible. They found two males tussling, one of them naked, and two women helping the smaller one resist. The uniforms settled things down in a hurry around the Oxford Apartments at 924 North Twenty-fifth Street. The police officers waved away the Milwaukee Fire Department rescue team, which had wrapped the young man in a blanket to cover his nakedness. Later reports would indicate that the officers thought the only blood they saw had resulted from a scraped knee.

With things under control, the police wanted to move the situation out of the public eye, away from the gathering crowd. They decided to head up to the apartment of the white man, who was trying to convince them that the naked young man was his lover. But the young women who had dialed the emergency number were not ready to give up so easily, and pestered the police to list them as witnesses. Sandra Smith said later they were told to go away, that they were no longer needed. They did, but when they returned home, upset and angry, they explained the episode to Glenda Cleveland, Sandra's mother, starting a domino effect that would take a bizarre turn. Glenda Cleveland followed up the excited discussion with a telephone call of her own to the police, a call that would eventually be broadcast around the world.

But for the moment, the police moved the two principals in the unfolding drama inside of the blocky apartment building and upstairs to apartment 213, the one pointed out by the slender white man with the wispy mustache. He continued his apologetic explanation, seemingly ashamed for being involved in such a ruckus. Since he spoke so calmly, the police officers began to feel that more important crimes were out there in the night, waiting to be thwarted. There were thieves and muggers, dope dealers and murderers who needed to be caught, and valuable time was being wasted standing here trying to referee what obviously amounted to nothing more than a domestic spat.

The tall man was glib and soft-spoken, not at all nervous, while the Asian guy seemed drunk and couldn't put together a coherent sentence. Whom to believe in this kind of situation? The tall guy admitted that he knew his Asian friend had been out on the street; that, he claimed, was why he had been trying to bring him back. It had happened before. They were homosexual lovers, he said, and they lived together in the apartment and tonight they had gotten to drinking a little too much and angry words were exchanged. He was really nineteen, much older than he looked. The man said he was sorry and that it wouldn't happen again. The police saw a few pictures of the younger man, apparently wearing only his underwear.

Konerak was terrified but could not articulate his case, propped up silently on the sofa while the men talked. The police seemed to be believing the tall man! What about the pictures that littered the floor and were tacked on the walls, photos that showed other naked men. Konerak had been raped! What of the smell that the tall man would tell investigators permeated the apartment from a corpse in the next room which he said had been smelling like hell when the three cops questioned him about the Asian kid.

But patrol work on the streets of a big city can put a coating of steel on normal human emotions. If a police officer takes every crime scene, every victim, every sob story too deeply and lets it get under his or her skin, then that is a cop who is likely to become another statistic in the suicide columns. Best to keep a distance. Settle things down, but don't let it get to you personally.

They established that the two were homosexual lovers, and cops who don't like to get involved in arguments between a man and wife just hate to get between a couple of arguing homosexuals. When police go into the homes of such people, they claim sometimes that pornographic books and pictures are the norm rather than an exception. Quiet things down and move on.

"What happened in Milwaukee, . . . that was normal, and I'll tell you why," a talk show-caller who described himself as a former paramedic told a Cleveland radio station. "Out of all of the calls that I went to, when there were gay people involved, okay, 95 percent of them, when you walked into the apartment, there was a strange odor. There was an exotic perfume or incense, there was, a lot of times, there were animal odors. I've been in places there was pornography, in boxes, stacked up to the windowsill. There were rows that you had to walk through because of the pornography. Tapes, movies, books, you just ignore that, you don't even see it."

The Milwaukee Police Association, the policemen's union, stated later that the officers on the scene found nothing to indicate anything was seriously wrong. As a matter of fact, things began to calm to such a point that the three officers did not feel it necessary to run a basic background check on either male they were questioning.

Had they done so, they would have learned some very interesting facts. They would have learned that the thirty-one-year-old white man, Jeffrey Lionel Dahmer, was convicted in 1989 of second-degree sexual assault on a teenage boy. They would have learned that Dahmer had done time for the crime and was still on probation. And they would have discovered that the Asian lad before them, the one who seemed too drunk to be understood, was only fourteen years old, not nineteen as Dahmer had claimed. And they would have learned that the boy was the younger brother of the child Dahmer had been convicted of molesting two years earlier. Dahmer had told the court during that 1989 case that he was sorry for what he had done, much as he was telling the police talking to him now that he was sorry, and that he would make sure that such an impolite interruption would not happen again.

The cops did not pick up their car radio microphones to call District Three headquarters and ask for the background checks, so they did not learn any of those things. Instead, they officially wrote it off as an argument between a couple of gays, got back into their cars, and drove away, off to patrol duties, back to serious crime.

The shiny badges going out the door, heading away from him, were the last things that Konerak Sinthasomphone would ever see as the door closed and Dahmer turned toward him, with those empty eyes and a face that was suddenly churning with anger.

11

When the cops got downstairs, they were somewhat amused by the interrogation they had just conducted, totally unaware of the horror that was going on in the very apartment where they had been standing moments before. One called in to the station to report. "Intoxicated Asian, naked male, was returned to his boyfriend." On a tape recording of the call, laughter was audible.

"My partner is going to get deloused at the station," the reporting officer said.

There was more laughter, and the two squad cars drove away.

CHAPTER TWO

The Infant Hercules

Summit County, Ohio, seems to have a private jinx that makes it a metropolitan also-ran. The favorite son is Wendell Willkie, who wasn't even born in Ohio, and when he carried the Republican banner in the 1940 presidential elections, he was trounced by Franklin Delano Roosevelt. However, he is still enshrined in brass on a courthouse wall in Akron. The favorite daughter is Judy Resnik, the brilliant kid out of Firestone High who became an astronaut, only to have the space shuttle *Challenger* blow up beneath her. Its most well-known institution of higher learning is the University of Akron, which pales in headlines when

13

compared with Kent State University, next door in Portage County, and even Kent State is more widely known as the place where national guardsmen slew students during Vietnam's turbulent years than for academic achievement.

The biggest city in Summit County is Akron, a decaying tooth of a metro area where empty storefronts stare out on Main Street. A merchant who was asked how business was didn't even look up while replying, "You didn't have to take a number to get in here, did you?" The county courthouse, a massive buff sandstone building in grand Second Renaissance Revival style, sits on a downtown hillock that is ironically called "the Gore." When the American automobile industry skidded into a ditch, it took Akron's rubber-making giants and the city economy with it.

In 1991, just when the area was fighting a recession and a drought, Summit County's long, rocky road got even rougher. Police investigators learned that it was here that Jeffrey Dahmer had killed his first victim, murdering Steven Hicks in a particularly gruesome manner that eventually would become a macabre trademark.

"The County of Summit—An Infant Hercules! Give him a wide berth, for he'll be a whopper." Such was the joyous toast that went up in 1840 when the Ohio legislature created the county by slicing sixteen townships from adjoining Portage, Medina, and Stark counties. The region was growing proudly, along with young America and the early industries that found a home here—canal boat building, pottery and glass makers, and grain and cereal mills—providing plenty of work. But the future arrived in 1870, in the form of young Dr. Benjamin Franklin Goodrich, who decided to set up a rubber-manufacturing plant along the hospitable banks of the Ohio Canal. At the time, there were ninety-four rubber plants in the nation, and the B.F. Goodrich Company was the only one in Ohio. As he turned out rubber hoses, brewery tubing, and cushions for pool tables, Goodrich also laid the groundwork for a miracle to come.

Over the years, his success attracted other entrepreneurs who were interested in making money and rubber by taking advantage of the empty factories left by the obsolete industries, whose time had passed, and in picking up as cheap labor the trainable men the closing businesses had laid off. Frank Seiberling bought seven Akron acres in 1898 and named his company after Charles Goodyear, the man who invented the vulcanization process, which gave rubber strength as well as elasticity. Harvey Firestone arrived in 1900 to create his own tire and rubber company, and five years later he made a deal with another young industrialist, named Henry Ford, to supply tires for all the motor cars Ford could produce. A boom was born.

Draw a line due northwest from the Pittsburgh steel mills and you reach Detroit, the car capital of the world. Halfway between them is busy Cleveland, with Akron twenty miles to the south, right on the trade routes for the transportation of raw material. Steel, rubber, and assembly lines. The formula that created mass-produced horseless carriages brought great wealth to the men who owned the factories, but it also showered money on ordinary workers. In 1910, there were only 69,067 people in Akron. By 1920, there were 208,435 living in the fastest-growing city in America. General Tire, Goodrich, Firestone, Goodyear, Mohawk, and others made Akron the Rubber Capital of the World. For a hundred years, rubber would dominate the city, although the jinx would hover around the edges.

Melwin Vaniman built a motor-powered airship in 1911 in Atlantic City, covered it with a coated fabric from Goodyear, and christened it the *Akron*. It exploded and crashed at sea. Twenty years later, the Goodyear Zeppelin Company constructed the largest thing in the sky, a 785-foot blimp, and named it, too, the *Akron*. After two years of excellent service, it crashed in the Atlantic Ocean, killing seventy-three people.

But the good times survived long enough to bring in hundreds of men from surrounding states to work in the rubber plants and make big money, money enough to buy fine silk shirts and perhaps a diamond ring for a girl back home. The "gummers," flush with money from their paychecks, would line up six deep at the bars, and the local burlesque house had to put on three shifts a day. Among the men who heard the call of opportunity was Willkie, a native of Elwood, Indiana, who worked for a time in the legal department of Firestone. He found the political world more to his liking because of Akron's economic roller coaster. The boom went bust after World War I and two-thirds of the men who had rushed to Akron for jobs were put out of work.

One such typical gummer was a teenager from a farm in Cadiz, Ohio, who abandoned the rural life in favor of a paycheck in the big city. The boy's name was Billy, and carrying only a straw suitcase, he arrived in the midst of the boom. Despite his lack of education, he soon found a job as a Firestone clerk and was making the princely sum of ninety-five dollars per month. The shy, hard working boy moved on to molding treads at the Miller Rubber Company's rim plant, and when the Depression hit, he found work in a clothing store until he was laid off there, too. Billy, clinging to the city, became fascinated with the Akron Music Hall, and hung around the actors so much that they gave him an unpaid job as a callboy and once even let him walk onstage and say, "Your cab has come, madame." When the Pauline McLean Players moved on because of the poor economic times, Billy was not asked to accompany them. Dejected, he headed for Tulsa to join his father in the oil fields. Later, he would try California, drop his first name of William, and just go by his middle and last names. Billy, who had a hard time even getting a blind date in Akron, became Clark Gable and did pretty well for himself in Hollywood. Akron has always had a problem keeping its young men around.

The great days, perhaps even the mediocre days, have now fled Akron. Downtown parking lots, even the one behind the Hilton Hotel, which is built around the Quaker Oats Company's old jumbo grain silos, still charge for parking, as if to discourage people from coming into town to shop. "Factories are laying off, downtown is laying off. Things are getting worse," observed a bank teller on the same day that the *Rubber & Plastics News,* required reading in the industry, ran a cartoon on its editorial page that showed a businessman on his knees in church, praying, "And Lord, please make people buy new cars." Akron's population stood at 275,425 in 1970. The 1990 census trimmed it down to 222,226.

But one undeniable benefit of the industrial boom days was that middle- and upper-level executives could find a nice life-style outside of the city, beyond the smog and the traffic and the crime. Unique little communities lured them to tranquil areas of rolling land, large old trees, acres of grass, and lots of privacy. Slide ten miles north of Akron on Interstate 77, take the Ghent Road exit west, cross Yellow Creek, and you are in one such idyllic place, a bucolic village called Bath Township.

Immediately, you will hit a crossroads that is the historic heart of the little town, where West Bath Road connects with the Cleve-Mass Road, once the main route connecting Cleveland with

Massillon, two cities about twenty miles equidistant from Bath. Interstate 77 now carries that through traffic, leaving the intersection at Bath Center to local vehicles and underlining the pleasant isolation that is enjoyed by the village. "This is a place where people come to live, not to work," said J. T. Norman, one of the township's three trustees. "Our zoning is committed to making this a rural, residential community." And it is just that.

Dominating the crossroads is the Bath Elementary School, a large block building that sits like a European fortress atop a knoll directly across the street from the wooden Bath Town Hall, a white plank structure that would be at home in New England. Occupying the corner to the right of the brick elementary school, on the downhill side of Bath Road, is the township's combined fire and police departments. In 1991, that crossroads would become a very busy place.

Drive between the school and the public safety buildings and you are on a narrow, undulating route that seems to take you back in time, maybe to the days when America was not a violent place. A brown, split-level home is tucked back in the trees at 4480 West Bath Road, and on May 17, 1968, the house got a new owner and family. Lionel Dahmer moved in along with Joyce, his wife of eight years, and their two sons, Jeffrey, aged seven, and David, one.

Lionel and Joyce Dahmer were married in Milwaukee on August 22, 1959, and moved into the downstairs flat of his mother's home in the quiet suburban community of West Allis, just over the city line. Jeffrey Lionel Dahmer, the couple's first child, was born on May 21, 1960, in Milwaukee's Evangelical Deaconess Hospital. Lionel was still attending college at the time, and he continued to commute to Marquette University on Wisconsin Avenue in downtown Milwaukee until he graduated in 1962 with a degree in electrical engineering.

After taking both a bachelor's and master's degree from Marquette, Lionel moved the family to Ames, Iowa, in the fall of 1962 and began a grueling Ph.D. study program at Iowa State University while at the same time supporting his wife and son. He finally earned his doctorate in analytical chemistry on November 19, 1966.

Joyce was pregnant again when he found employment as a chemist with PPG Industries and the family moved again, this time to Doylestown, Ohio, a blue-collar area on the outskirts of Akron. Jeffrey's brother, David, was born a few months later, on December 18. Lionel and Joyce started looking toward the future, and began shopping for a bigger house and a pleasant place for the boys to grow up. It didn't take too many visits to the beautiful environs of Bath Township to convince them that the little town under the trees would be a great place in which to put down their own roots. A year later they moved to Bath, feeling fortunate to be able to finally land in such a tranquil area.

The forest can be a magical place for a boy, and the house in Bath Township was right in the middle of one. There were other houses around, but one thing the hamlet has in abundance is trees. In summer, tall trees in full bloom jam so tightly together that many of the township's roads are little more than shady tunnels of leaves. In such a place, imaginations can grow and a boy who is shy and turns inward can lose himself for hours in the woods, watching animals, tracking, learning. It can be nice to be alone. No one tells you what to do when you are by yourself. Seclusion can be a refuge for a child, particularly when things happening at home are unpleasant and especially when a little boy has no playmates.

But it is always hard for a kid coming into a new community. For Jeffrey, who turned eight on May 21, four days after his father purchased the new home, it was even more difficult than usual. He was alone, with no friends whatsoever. He had attended the first and second grades in Doylestown, but any boyhood chums from there were far, far away. His little brother was just a baby. Summer had just begun, so school was out and other kids were already scattered. Jeffrey found himself on his own.

Later in life, after Jeffrey began getting into serious trouble, Lionel Dahmer would telephone a probation officer and divulge a disturbing piece of information. When Jeffrey was eight, his father said, a neighborhood boy had sexually molested him. Perhaps that "may be the reason why

Jeffrey has problems with sexuality issues," the probation officer wrote on her official report for April 27, 1990. To experts, childhood molestation is a red flag, one possible origin of a troubled adulthood. But in all of the early records of the case, this was the sole mention of Jeffrey being molested, something that Dahmer himself vehemently denied. An eight-year-old boy, feeling alone in a strange new place, could have been easy prey for someone who chose to befriend him in the woods.

School days finally began and Jeffrey had an opportunity to begin mingling with children his own age, first on the short bus rides on West Bath Road, and later in the classes at elementary school. One youngster, who shared that ride in the yellow bus with Jeffrey every morning, remembered him as being funny and kind of odd at the same time. Although tall for his age, Jeff would not bully smaller classmates, but at the same time, if one were hurt, his reaction was to laugh, not help. Even as a youngster he had begun to pull back from others. And like many children, even among today's generation, he was fascinated by the mystical nature of things, particularly about how things lived, and how they died.

While his classmates were having a difficult time connecting with him, adults liked Jeffrey. He was polite, neat, and willing to please, flashing a gentle, shy smile when he was complimented. Georgia Scharenberg, who lived next door, recalled Jeff as being "a nice boy" who spent his out-of-school hours prowling in the woods, climbing the stony ledges and dashing among the trees. There were few playmates, she said. "Jeff was more or less with his brother all the time, and not with the other boys." Other grown-ups who knew the child concurred that if anything marked Jeffrey's behavior in childhood, it was his sense of politeness and good manners.

In the same way that Akron cannot keep its young men, Jeffrey Dahmer had a hard time keeping friends. By the time he hit junior high school, the overpowering loneliness that was to haunt his existence was already showing like an ominous banner, identifying the skinny, tow-headed kid with the big glasses as being different. Mrs. Scharenberg, who worked as a cashier in the lunchroom of Eastview Junior High School, recalled that when the boy came through the line, they would usually exchange a few remarks at the register before Jeffrey carried his tray away. He would sit down with other students at a table to eat, but when he left the room, he always left alone.

In one remarkable break from his pattern, Jeffrey did begin reaching out to people. While still in junior high, he got a job selling shrubbery for a local nursery. He ran over to the Scharenbergs' home with a catalog and, bubbling with enthusiasm, talked them into buying two apple trees and a yellow bush that would flower in the spring. It didn't take much talking, because the couple enjoyed helping out the neighborhood kids. The trees and bush took root and even today continue growing out in the woods that border their property (though they never did get any apples from those apple trees).

By the time his junior high days were finished, Jeffrey apparently had made a vital discovery. He had tasted alcohol for the first time and began to believe its soothing song. For a boy bogged down in melancholy moods, everything seemed a bit more rosy when he could tip back a swig or two of gin from the bottles he would hide. Life was easier. At about fourteen years of age, Jeffrey Dahmer was already taking the dark road into alcoholism, not just sipping alcoholic beverages as many underage youths do, but actually drinking to get drunk.

Something else was going on in his life, too, something in the woods behind the brown house, something that even Jeffrey probably didn't comprehend. At about the age of ten, he had begun to experiment with things that were once alive, bleaching the bones of dead chickens, stuffing insects into bottles of formaldehyde, and decapitating small rodents. It was an interesting hobby to him, and a pastime that left its mark and would grow right along with him. Through trial and error, he learned to use acid to help strip the meat off of the bones of dead animals. It became almost second nature to him. It was not unusual for people to find the bones of animals among the leaves and vines in the woods off West Bath Road.

In 1975, when Jeff was in high school, three neighborhood youngsters were tramping through the woods behind the Dahmer home when they stumbled across what was left of a dog. The head had been cut off and the gutted carcass was dangling from a tree behind a cross made of sticks. The kids who found it would recall in later years that it looked like the remnants of devil worship. No one ever connected the carcass to the actions of any individual.

By his senior year at Revere High School, Jeffrey Dahmer had learned a few things: he could drink with the best of them, and he discovered that getting attention was easy. People would watch you if you were willing to do strange things. The consensus among his classmates was that he was one weird dude who knew no bounds in reaching out to get a laugh, to snatch a bit of spotlight for an instant. Like over at the Summit Mall, when he would go into his "retarded" act and stumble and flap around, throwing those long arms in the air and tumbling over people carrying packages and eating food. That was always good for a couple of laughs. He would take any dare. People liked him when he did strange things.

Little was sacred to him by that time. When the pictures were taken for the yearbook in his senior year, 1978, Jeff had a surprise for the eggheads in the school. Members of the National Honor Society, an elite group of students with high grade-point averages and records of community service, gathered on the school steps to be photographed for the *Minutemen,* a slick annual with a scarlet cover. A nonmember edged in at the last minute. When the shutter clicked, right smack in the middle of the group, third from the top, was Jeffrey Dahmer. What a riot! When word got around that Jeff, with his less than 2.0 average, had sneaked in among the NHS geeks, there was great appreciation from those who would never come close to that kind of scholastic achievement. The story didn't quite end there, however, because people do not get into the Honor Society by being stupid. The yearbook editor simply took an ink brush and blacked out the face and body of the intruder. In a photograph of forty-five students, Jeffrey Dahmer literally became the Boy Who Wasn't There. Invisible, even in a crowd, and clearly unwanted.

He played it for laughs, but psychiatrists and legal experts many years later would examine that single picture closely. By that time, it would be determined that Jeffrey Dahmer had a high IQ, that despite grades that fluctuated from A to F in school, he possessed a brain that easily could have qualified him for that special group of students, had he only been willing to work to obtain that goal. They would point out that Jeff had not snuck into the picture of the tennis team, or the glee club, but only into the shot of the National Honor Society, perhaps where he felt he really belonged. Membership would have made his parents proud of him, the experts observed. Perhaps

Jeff, already being kept at arm's length by his classmates, did not want to show off his intelligence and chose to be perceived as an unthreatening dullard, someone who would be easy to like.

His senior picture in the same yearbook, at the bottom of page 145, shows a youngster with full blond hair that dips low across his forehead. He is wearing narrow wire-rimmed glasses, a print shirt open at the collar, and a dark jacket. Except for the somewhat soulful expression on his long face, he looks exactly like any other high school student might, and certainly no different from the other 255 members of his graduating class. To the right side of the page is his school biography: "JEFF DAHMER: Band 1; *Lantern* 3; Tennis Intramurals 2, 3, 4; Ohio State Univ. (Business) . . ."

Again, the dim path followed by a loner can be seen clearly in hindsight. His work on the *Lantern,* the student newspaper, allowed him to be an individual in the middle of a group. Tennis also is a one-on-one game, not requiring teamwork. In a band, a person plays a single instrument, but since that also required him to be part of a disciplined unit, he apparently decided not to pursue it beyond the ninth grade.

For the class of '78, it was a fun year, although they didn't finish the homecoming float until just a few hours before they had to display it. The yearbook editors noted that the fun things included the Michael Stanley Band, hanging out at the SkyWay and Whitney's, hitting the mall when

27

nothing better was happening, "fluffy parties," concerts at Blossom and the Coliseum, and visits to haunted houses. What was not mentioned was the senior class trip to Washington, D.C., a trip during which Jeff proved his mettle as a prankster to impress his classmates.

While the rest of the seniors made the usual tourist stops at the Washington Monument and the Smithsonian and trekked up to Capitol Hill, Jeff hit the telephones. Using the charm that he could summon when needed and a bit of midwestern twang, and by laying a guilt trip on a governmental aide, Dahmer engineered a visit for himself and his pals to the Office of the Vice-President of the United States of America. Walter Mondale wasn't in at the time, but the group had a good time anyway. Then Jeff got them in to see the office of Art Buchwald, the writer who coats his satire with humorous barbs. The seniors carried the tale back to Revere High School with them, and other classmates shook their heads in amazement. They were used to Jeffrey's antics by this time and tended to brush off his outrageous behavior by saying he was just "doing a Dahmer." Standing on the periphery, they could enjoy it. They just didn't want to get too close to his flame. After all, someone who drank so much and liked to trace bodies on the schoolroom floor with chalk just *had* to be a little bit more than odd.

One person decided to take a chance on him. When he asked sixteen-year-old Bridget Geiger to be his date for the senior prom, she accepted because she knew that while he acted crazy around his pals, he was usually shy with girls. He promised her that he would neither drink nor act strange during their date, but he was still quite uncomfortable in his role as polite escort of a cute girl in a prom dress. Instead of a tux, Jeff wore a pair of neat dark pants, a vest, and a slender bow tie. And he was nervous, perhaps afraid that Bridget might kiss him.

The evening didn't work out as planned. Jeff left the dance for about an hour, and the chaperons would not let him back in because they thought he might have alcoholic beverages on him. He insisted that he had only stepped out for a burger and fries. He and Bridget, along with two friends, left and spent the rest of the evening at a nearby pub, where they drank sodas and talked.

That date was followed a few weeks later by Jeff inviting her to a party at the Dahmer home on West Bath Road. Geiger described the event as a rather ordinary kind of social with only a few people around. Ordinary, that is, until the point in the evening when the group decided to have a séance. Everyone got comfortable and in a séance kind of mood. The lights were turned off. Then someone—she says it was not Jeffrey—had an idea: the group should contact Satan. Just then, the trembling flames on the candles snapped. That was enough for a good Catholic girl. She got up and left the party. She would not see Jeffrey Dahmer again until pictures and stories about him started popping up everywhere thirteen years later.

Still somewhat sympathetic to the oddball in her senior class, Geiger contends that it's no wonder Dahmer became so screwed up. Everyone was always picking on him at school and he would never fight back; he just internalized the hurt and laughed it off. He might have laughed, but he would not forget. When he eventually took his revenge, it would be on others, but it would be fearful and mighty and far beyond the ken of schoolyard bullies. No one would ever again black out his picture.

CHAPTER THREE

First Blood

June 1978

Something else was preying on the mind of Jeffrey Dahmer during his senior year in high school, something that apparently had an electrifying effect on his behavior. His parents were going through a divorce that turned mean. Many years later he would confide to a probation officer how deeply he was disturbed by the rancor in his home.

"Would you describe your early childhood (prior to adolescence) as happy or unhappy?" Donna Chester asked him, reading from a printed form. "Not happy," he replied. Beneath the remark, the probation officer wrote in her shorthand notes, "fighting parent [*sic*]."

Then she followed up with, "If you could change anything about your childhood, what would you change?" The official answer checked on the probation form read, "dissatisfied with family, self or emotional climate." Chester's accompanying comment declared that Jeffrey would "change that parent [*sic*] didn't get along."

Dahmer said he had "mixed or neutral" feelings toward both his mother and his father and that he was never abused by his parents, who limited their discipline during his teenage years to a scolding, taking away some privileges, or grounding him by not letting him leave the house. He added that his parents would have described him as a good, normal kid and that he viewed himself as just an average guy.

Lionel and Joyce Dahmer lived together, for the most part, from the time they were married in 1959 until shortly before the divorce decree was granted on July 24, 1978. That year, that very summer when the arguments were cresting, turned out to be the most momentous time in the life of their son Jeffrey, until 1991 came along and the world, as he knew it, ground to a halt.

Lionel, the Ph.D. chemist advancing in his career at PPG Industries, and Joyce, with only her high school education, had watched their marriage slowly fall to pieces, like a thunderstorm that gathers bit by bit on a distant horizon, at first issuing low rumbles of noise, but accelerating and growing until flashes of lightning and booming thunder envelop everything in the storm's path. Before Lionel moved out, taking lodging in a nearby motel on the Cleve-Mass Road, he was stringing a trip wire tagged with keys that would rattle if someone approached while he slept.

By the time the first legal papers were filed in the Summit County Court of Common Pleas before Judge Richard V. Zurz in late 1977, things had gotten bad and were getting worse. Lionel filed first and then Joyce answered back, both charging extreme cruelty and gross neglect. As Divorce Action 77-11-4162 grew thicker in its manila file folder, there would be repeated references to Joyce's mental condition.

Her lawyer declared in one hearing that Lionel was harassing Joyce "to the point where he, once again, was just about intent upon driving Mrs. Dahmer back to the psychiatrist." His lawyer would refer in an objection to the "extensive mental illness" of the defendant, Joyce.

While the marital storm roiled above him, Jeffrey tried to keep his head above water at school. Christmas of 1977 was not the most pleasant in the Dahmer household. He began drinking heavily, seeking solace on his own, in a stupor. His dependence on alcohol was known to most of his acquaintances and they kept a distance from him, as if divorce were the flu and alcoholism akin to a common cold that could be passed on to someone else.

The legalisms continued to fly like daggers between Joyce, Lionel, and their lawyers. Finally, Judge Zurz cut a deal and granted the divorce in July. Joyce got custody of the "minor child"— David—along with $225 a month in support and maintenance, $400 a month in alimony for six years, and an additional $125 per month if she was attending college. She also got half of the shares that Lionel had purchased in PPG stock, the family's ten-year-old Oldsmobile Cutlass, and title to a part of the house on West Bath Road. She agreed to quitclaim the house over to Lionel when he came up with $23,500 for her share. Lionel, who desperately wanted to have custody of his youngest son, drove away instead with their 1972 Ford station wagon and his freedom. He would soon be back in the house.

Only five months after the ink dried on the divorce, Lionel wed again, marrying his second wife, Shari, herself a divorcée of four years, on the day before Christmas, 1978. He was forty-two. She was thirty-seven. Joyce took back her maiden name, Flint, to erase Lionel from her name as well as her life.

Even with the court work done, parting was not an easy thing for Joyce and Lionel. Two years later, Joyce would summon police to the three-bedroom home in Bath Township, claiming that Lionel and she had argued again and that he had attacked her both with angry words and with his

34

hands. Police quieted the event and reported no signs of injury. No charges were ever filed.

The continuing link between Joyce and Lionel was their younger boy, David, who bound them together throughout this most traumatic part of their relationship like a patch of super glue. Both wanted the boy and fought long and hard through their lawyers to keep him. The child custody battles that began in 1978, when David was only twelve, continued for years in searing, bitter legal confrontations. Though Joyce originally got custody, over the years, that changed. David decided to live with his father.

Sitting on the sidelines throughout the wrenching event, feeling totally left out as his home life shattered, was Jeffrey, feeling forsaken as his parents battled over David. By a quirk of the calendar, he turned eighteen years of age on May 21 of 1978, just in time for his high school graduation and two months before the divorce was final. The law suddenly didn't look at him very hard, and when the divorce was granted, it was claimed that because of his of age and educational stature, Jeffrey was what is termed "emancipated." Translated into everyday English, that meant that he was considered a grown-up in the eyes of the court, an adult male who was able to fend for himself. This tall, lanky, excruciatingly shy young man, who was unable to hold his own in the male world and was already a closet drunk, suddenly was *grown!* Right. And elephants can fly.

Silent rage built to white heat within him. It appeared to Jeffrey that, once again, nobody wanted him. His father had moved out and both of his parents seemed to want only David, because that was whom they were fighting over. The court wasn't the least bit interested in him; in the stack of court documents surrounding the divorce, Jeffrey was hardly mentioned at all. He had graduated from Revere High on June 4, and what few acquaintances he had would be departing for colleges and jobs and the real world. A sense of impending loneliness settled on him like a dark shroud.

Years later, police and psychiatrists would say that the paramount thing that triggered Dahmer's towering, murderous rage was simply not wanting people to leave him. If you tried to leave, you died.

The brown house at 4480 West Bath Road underwent an appraisal during the divorce proceedings. The data that was submitted by appraiser Tom Conway stated that the modern style timber and concrete home was located on 1.72 irregular acres. He reported that a wood porch ran along the eastern side of the stone over block residence that also had a separate two-car garage that was reached over a gravel driveway. The 250 by 300 foot lot slopes down west to east and water is gathered from the runoff by a spring which services the home.

Inside, Conway reported that the house had a

living room, a dining room, a family room, a kitchen and a utility room, along with two full bathrooms and three bedrooms. A small room adjacent to the living room contained a hot water tank and an oil-fired boiler. But the appraiser was not impressed with the upkeep of the place, saying the house needed some maintenance, both inside and outside. On March 20, 1978, he rated it as having a fair market value of about $58,000. Like other homes in that much-desired area, its value would appreciate substantially over the next dozen years. Surrounding properties, even some vacant lots, were selling for six figures.

This was the house that, after signing the divorce papers, Lionel Dahmer walked up to one day with a child support check in his hand. According to court documents, he claimed that Joyce "came out and said, 'You got everything,' and started hitting me on the chest."

And this was the house in which Jeffrey Dahmer, an angry young man devastated by his past and frightened about his future, found himself alone on the night of June 18, 1978. Joyce and David were visiting relatives in Chippewa Falls, Wisconsin, and his father was already out of the house. He decided to do something about his situation. He would go out and get himself a friend.

Steven M. Hicks, nineteen, from nearby Coventry Township, was, like Jeffrey Dahmer, tall and lean at five feet eleven and 160 pounds. Unlike Jeffrey, he had a lot of friends. Four days shy of his nineteenth birthday, he had gone out for a day of summer fun. While hitchhiking along Ohio Route 224, he was picked up at about 11:00 A.M. by a convoy of friends, who ferried him up to Chippewa Lake Park in Medina County, right next door to Summit County, to attend a rock music concert.

They spent much of the day together, soaking up the rays and getting into the music, and when his pals left, Hicks promised to rendezvous with them later at the old airport landing strip near Lockwood Corners. He would get there, he said, the same way he had gotten to the park, by sticking out his thumb and catching a ride. Steve Hicks was a trusting soul.

Wearing blue jeans, a necklace chain with a red cross on it, and blue tennis shoes, Steve Hicks had another reason to return home. It was his father's birthday and he wanted to present a gift to him when the family threw a party that night.

So there he was, standing alongside the Cleve-Mass Road, looking for a ride, when this tuna boat of an Olds Cutlass pulled over. A guy about his own age was at the wheel. Jeff Dahmer flashed a big smile. Hey, he told his passenger, I'm all by myself over at my house. Dad doesn't live there anymore, and Mom and my brother are visiting relatives in Wisconsin. Let's go have a few beers and listen to some music. There was probably a promise to give him a ride to the landing strip later.

A sharp turn on West Bath, between the police

station and the elementary school, and they scooted on down to the 4400 block, turning left at the telephone pole and grinding up the gravel driveway to the house. They got to know each other and they drank beer and talked. Jeff was fresh out of Revere and Steve was graduating from Coventry High. The music was loud and the good times, for Jeff, were rolling. He really liked this guy, tall like himself and with long brown hair that fell below his neck in back and covered his ears. The face was sensitive, and when Steve smiled, the room lit up. Despite the instant relationship, Dahmer told police that sex was not part of the evening.

Then Steve made the worst mistake he had ever made in his life, and it would be his last one. He looked at the clock and decided it was time to go. No, said Jeff. Yes, said Steve. "The guy wanted to leave and I didn't want him to leave," Dahmer would tell police thirteen years later while describing this cataclysmic event in his young life.

Jeffrey picked up a dumbbell and smashed it into the head of Steven Hicks and the boy went down like a crumpling blanket. Bath Township Police Lieutenant Richard Munsey, after interviewing Dahmer in 1991, wrote in the unvarnished terminology of a policeman's report that "Mr. Dahmer indicated that in 1978 he picked up a hitchhiker at the Cleveland-Massillon Road and Bath Road, Bath Township, Summit County, Ohio. Mr. Dahmer and the hitchhiker returned to Mr. Dahmer's residence at 4480 West Bath Road and Mr. Dahmer struck the hitchhiker over the head with a barbell and strangled him to death. Mr. Dahmer dismembered the body in his residence and buried the body on his property outside his residence. He then dug up the body and Mr. Dahmer then broke up the bones and scattered the bones. The bones were scattered over the property lines of 4480 West Bath Road; 4410 West Bath Road, and 4464 West Bath Road." The last address listed is the home of Elmer and Georgia Scharenberg, the couple that had befriended young Jeffrey Dahmer, let him play in their yard, and bought from him shrubbery they didn't need and a couple of barren apple trees. Near those trees Jeffrey would scatter the bones of Steven Hicks.

Once he had killed Hicks in front of the bookshelves in the den, Dahmer hauled the body outside, around to a crawl space beneath the house. There he picked up a long knife and used the knowledge he had gained in slicing up animals to dismember the boy with whom he had been partying a few minutes earlier, exerting final control over the new friend he had found. The various parts were stuffed into plastic garbage bags, which were hidden in the crawl space. After a few days of summer heat, the flesh and organs began to decompose; a nauseating smell became noticeable as the dismembered human parts began to bake in the plastic as if in a pressure cooker. The episode was becoming ever more risky for him, for while he was alone, his mother would eventually return and his father might stop over at any time. Neighbors and nosy children could pay an unexpected, unwanted visit. Jeffrey was forced to make another decision, and he first chose to haul the parts away, then reversed himself and decided to bury them, only to be foiled by the hard, rocky soil. He managed to scoop out a shallow gave, dump his victim in, and cover up the hole.

Within days, a quiver of panic erupted in his chest as Dahmer worried that the grave might be discovered by kids playing in the woods. They might notice something was different, just as he used to know every branch and root back there and could spot when anything had changed. The grave might stand out too much. He dug up the bags.

Then he went to work in earnest, putting sweat into his labors. He carefully peeled the flesh from the bones and, picking up a sledgehammer, began cracking them into little pieces, one by one. When he finished hours later, no bone fragment existed that was larger than a person's hand. As his final task, he disposed of the decayed flesh and then climbed onto a sharp, rocky ledge behind the house. Turning slowly in a circle, he cast the bone fragments into the forest in a macabre shower, making a full 360-degree revolution, around and around, like a farmer tossing chicken feed, until he had nothing left to throw away. He was a sorcerer making magic, spreading the remains of Steven Hicks so that no one would ever put him back together again. But with the bones in the backyard, Steve would, in a sense, always be there for him.

He was now a murderer and a sadist, but at least there was one person who had not left Jeffrey Dahmer without paying the price. The killings would continue for thirteen more years, and before all was said and done, Jeffrey would kill a total of seventeen times. If they thought they could leave, he would prove that he could keep them around for as long as he wanted. He was in control! And his choice, time and again, would be that they would *never* leave him. Jeffrey destroyed Hicks's wallet in a fire and threw the incriminating knife and the necklace Steve had worn off the bridge on West Bath Road, hurling them into the deep waters of the Cuyahoga River.

Richard and Martha Hicks filed a missing persons report on their son a few days later, but as time passed, hope slowly dimmed. Then it, too, died, the file in the drawer beside the police department's coffee machine lingering uselessly. The disappearance of Steven Hicks became the only unsolved missing person case in Summit County.

Just when Jeffrey may have thought he had solved the problem of abandonment, he got another dose of reality, learning just how alone a person truly could be.

With the court's permission, Lionel Dahmer dropped by the house in late August to visit his boys, and an agitated Jeffrey answered the door. According to Lionel, Jeffrey told his father that Joyce and David weren't there. They had gone away again to Chippewa Falls and this time were not coming back; they had decided to live with relatives. His mother had told him not to tell his father, and although things were getting grim around the house, until that moment he had kept that promise.

Not only had Jeffrey been left alone, but according to his stepmother he had no money and only a little food was left in the refrigerator, which was broken. Lionel and Shari moved in, and Jeffrey lived with them until it was time for him to go off to college, down to Ohio State University in Columbus.

CHAPTER FOUR

911

Monday, May 27, 1991, 2:30 A.M.

In a tale bereft of the usual sort of heroes, the actions of Glenda Cleveland, her daughter, Sandra Smith, and her niece, Nicole Childress, stand out in bold relief. The school system, the United States Army, and the officialdom of justice in Ohio and Milwaukee had failed to heed the storm flags that Jeffrey Dahmer had been waving for years. The three women were apparently the first to actually stand in his path and say, "No."

When Sandra and Nicole hurried to Cleveland's neat flat, not far from the Oxford Apartments in which grisly things were taking place at that early-morning hour, they were upset, talking fast. The story spilled out of them as they talked, stepping on each other's words in their haste to describe their adventure. Cleveland let them talk, knowing they would eventually get through it. But she did not like what she had heard so far.

The girls had been out on Twenty-fifth, they said, when they saw that little Laotian kid stumbling about "butt naked," like he was hurt. They saw blood on his naked buttocks and legs and the boy was mumbling incoherently when they reached him. The boy would fall down every time he tried to stand up. Then that tall man came up, carrying some beer he had bought over on Twenty-seventh Street, and saw what was happening. When he tried to pull the boy away, twisting him by the arm, the girls called for help and a pair of police cars and a fire engine rolled quickly to the scene, and a crowd began to gather. Then the police took over and walked the man and the kid back to the Oxford Apartments. When Sandra and Nicole told the officers they were witnesses and wanted to have their names taken down in case testimony was needed, the cops told them to go away.

Glenda Cleveland, thirty-seven, hails from a family of nine kids in Carthage, Mississippi, a place she left eighteen years ago, looking for work. She was an unwed mother carrying her baby, Sandra, who has recently given birth to a son of her own, making Cleveland a grand-

46

mother, a role in which she rejoices. Coming from such a family, she has a strong protective streak where children are concerned. A slender, soft-spoken woman who pulls her hair back away from her face and watches the world through large, plastic-rimmed glasses, Cleveland works as a typesetter for the C.P. Gauger Company in Milwaukee and she believes in taking care of business.

So when the girls finished their story, she realized that something bad might have happened to that Laotian boy, a child that she knew. He was just a baby! She decided to get involved herself and dialed the police emergency code, 911.

She was polite, but not awed, when talking to the police. Being persistent in tracking down someone who knew about the incident, she remained steady to her inquiry when one of the officers who had investigated the incident finally picked up a telephone to talk to her. It wasn't until she realized that her call was not going to send police back out to investigate further that her voice began to shake.

A transcript of that ill-fated telephone conversation reads this way:

911 OPERATOR: Milwaukee Emergency Operator 55. May I help you?

CLEVELAND: Yes, yes. A moment ago, how long ago was it? About 10 minutes ago, my daughter and my niece flagged down a policeman when they walked up on a young child being molested by a male guy and, uh, no information or anything was taken, but they were taken downtown. I was wondering, I mean, I'm sure further information must be needed. The boy was naked and bleeding.

911 OPERATOR: O.K.

CLEVELAND: Have you had any reports of that? Anyone been brought down like that?

911 OPERATOR: O.K., you know where it happened at?

CLEVELAND: The squad car was Number 68 that they flagged down and they picked him up.

911 OPERATOR: Um hunh.

CLEVELAND: And my daughter and my niece said, that, you know, their names or nothing was taken down or whatnot, but the fact is that a crime was being committed, I'm sure you must need, you know, some kind of information based on it.

911 OPERATOR: O.K. Let me get you someone to talk to.

CLEVELAND: O.K.

[She is put on hold momentarily until another voice answers.]

OPERATOR: 66.

CLEVELAND: I was calling to see if a squad car, Number 68, brought someone in, a child being molested by an adult that was witnessed by my daughter and my niece?

OPERATOR: Where was this?

CLEVELAND: 26th and Highland, Sandra? 25th and State. O.K., they was the ones that witnessed it and flagged the policeman down, and you know, told about the situation, but their names or nothing was taken down, and I'm wondering if this situation was being handled. Because what it indicated was that this was a male child being raped and molested by an adult. It was . . .

OPERATOR: Where did this happen?

CLEVELAND: Around 25th and State.

OPERATOR: O.K., now what district were you calling?

CLEVELAND: What district? They were flagged down. The policemen were flagged down.

OPERATOR: O.K. If that's where it happened, then they were in that district. Hang on one second.

CLEVELAND: O.K.

[She is put on hold a second time while the call is transferred once again.]

OPERATOR: District Three.

CLEVELAND: Yes. I was wondering earlier this evening about 15 minutes ago, my daughter and my niece flagged down a squad car, Number 68, whereas they witnessed a young child being molested by an adult.

OPERATOR: Um hunh.

CLEVELAND: And has this been reported?

OPERATOR: Where was this happening at?

CLEVELAND: 25th and State.

OPERATOR: 25th and State.

CLEVELAND: Yes.

OPERATOR: Hold on. Let me check.

CLEVELAND: O.K.

49

[She is put on hold for a third time and the call is transferred to a specific police officer's telephone.]

OFFICER: Police.

CLEVELAND: Yes. There was a squad car Number 68 that was flagged down here earlier this evening, about 15 minutes ago.

OFFICER: That was me.

CLEVELAND: Yeah. What happened? I mean my daughter and my niece witnessed what was going on. Was anything done about this situation? Do they need their names, or . . .

OFFICER: No, I don't need them.

CLEVELAND: Or information, or anything from them?

OFFICER: No, not at all.

CLEVELAND: You don't?

OFFICER: Nope. It was an intoxicated boyfriend of another boyfriend.

CLEVELAND: Well, how old was this child?

OFFICER: It wasn't a child. It was an adult.

CLEVELAND: Are you sure?

OFFICER: Yup.

CLEVELAND: Are you positive? Because this child doesn't even speak English. My daughter has dealt with him before, seen him on the street, you know . . .

OFFICER: Yeah. No, uh, he's uh, he's . . . It's all taken care of, Ma'am.

CLEVELAND: Isn't this . . . I mean, what if he's a child and not an adult? I mean, are you positive this is an adult?

OFFICER: Ma'am. Ma'am. Like I explained to you, it's as positive as I can be.

CLEVELAND: Oh. I see . . .

OFFICER: I can't do anything about someone's sexual preferences in life, and if . . .

CLEVELAND: Well, no, I'm not saying anything about that, but it appeared to have been a child, this is why . . .

OFFICER: No.

CLEVELAND: No?

OFFICER: No, he's not.

Despite the fruitless results of her conversation with the Milwaukee police, Cleveland was not ready to dismiss the situation from her mind, feeling that the Laotian boy could be in jeopardy. Four days after calling 911, she read a newspaper article concerning the disappearance of Konerak Sinthasomphone and decided to go one step higher in her effort to alert authorities. This time, she telephoned the Federal Bureau of Investigation.

The FBI telephoned the Police Department and inquired about the report on a missing person, apparently deciding that since no evidence existed that a federal crime had been committed, the local authorities should handle the matter.

The Milwaukee police returned a call to Glenda Cleveland, saying they were aware of the incident and would contact her. She waited. No one came to talk.

It would be learned in a few months that her

efforts would have been to no avail in any case, even if the police had come zooming back to apartment 213 with sirens wailing and lights flashing. The fatal mistake already had been made. A quick response at that point would have done nothing to help Konerak.

Dahmer, in discussing the matter, told investigators that as soon as the door closed and the three police officers walked back downstairs, he had strangled the drugged Laotian boy until he was dead.

Dahmer said he then had sex with the corpse, took some photographs to add to his horrible collection, and began the long process of dismembering the body. As a trophy, he chose to keep the teenager's skull.

Konerak Sinthasomphone was one more person who would never leave Jeffrey Dahmer.

CHAPTER FIVE

The Green Machine

January 12, 1979—March 26, 1981

Private First Class Dahmer, Jeffrey L., stretched out his full six-foot length on the wool blanket covering the thin mattress of his steel bunk and reached for his tunes and his briefcase. It was Friday night and his work for the week was done. It was snowing on the German plains and the temperatures outside were frigid. The weekend was his and he intended to spend it right where he was, indoors, warm in his rack and stone drunk.

Liquor was forbidden in the U.S. Army barracks, of course, but a smart dude could always get around regulations and PFC Dahmer was more than just a smart dude. He popped the snaps on the briefcase and it flipped apart, laying out before him a mini-bar complete with stirrers, shakers, martini glasses, and a bottle of gin. When inspections were held, the sergeants would check that his bed had hospital corners and the uniforms were clean and the hangers were spaced two finger widths apart, that the footlocker was neat and that things were generally squared away, the army way. They never opened the briefcase, for that would have been prying into a man's private domain.

In Baumholder, Germany, the brass wanted to keep the GIs happy, for these young warriors would be on the cutting edge if the Russian and Warsaw Pact tanks ever started to roll over the NATO-protected fields of West Germany. In that period of recent history, the Cold War was still a very hot item. So they were willing to cut the boys a little slack on the unimportant stuff. If PFC Dahmer could be a model soldier during inspection, and do his job at the infirmary come Monday morning, he could keep his booze handy. He would not be the first nor the last GI to stash a bottle in a barracks or a desk drawer for use on a cold night in Germany.

Dahmer had joined up after dropping out of Ohio State following a single brief and boozy quarter. The big university in nearby Columbus opened its doors to the children of Ohio who managed to hang on to a passing grade average in high school, and Jeffrey had made it in by the skin of his teeth. Columbus was a welcome move out of Bath, particularly after the night he went out with an acquaintance to do a bit of hell-raising, only to be confronted in a driveway by an angry resident carrying a gun. Police had checked out the report, but Jeffrey and his cohort were not arrested.

At Ohio State, enrolled in the basic courses that all freshmen must endure, Dahmer had stumbled into the Land of the Keg Party. College students, as a rule, like to drink, and the newly emancipated Jeffrey Dahmer was not going to swim against that tide. Soon, bottles lined the shelves of his room and he was smuggling bottles into the classrooms to help him make it through the lectures. He went into Ohio State in September and came out in December and shortly thereafter was escorted by his newly remarried father to the office of an army recruiter.

Jeffrey had killed a man on June 18, his father and mother had divorced on July 24, he had thoroughly wasted the fall quarter at Ohio State and dropped out of college in December, his father, had remarried on Christmas Eve, 1978, and five days after that Jeff signed up for the army. Christmas, traditionally a time for families to rejoice in togetherness, was for Jeffrey Dahmer a time of intense internal turmoil. His mother and brother had left in August and the family, as he had known it, no longer existed.

Through a tough program of discipline, hard work, and training, Uncle Sam had straightened out many a troubled young man and now he would have a chance to put Jeffrey Dahmer on the right path. Uncle Sam was going to lose this particular confrontation.

Despite the Ohio State fiasco, Dahmer came to be considered a bright guy in the all-volunteer army. Although he was only a PFC, consistently staying right down there with the beginning ranks, his army buddies marveled at the way he could devour books as well as brews. They guessed his IQ to be around 145, which would be on the genius level, because he read so much. But it was noted also that some of his favorite books were children's classic fairy tales of trolls and goblins.

He was a hard one to figure out. During bull sessions, he would talk about how hard he was working to please his father, but generally he would keep to himself, at least when he was sober.

The near-genius was a mystery to the men of the Second Battalion of the U.S. Army's Sixty-eighth Armored Regiment of the Eighth Infantry Division, Mechanized. Here was a soldier who wore the uniform with pride, who had all these brains, was a good medic, and who was going nowhere fast. Occasionally, he would take off for town and get a whore, and there was never a hint of homosexuality, but he would also spend many a weekend right there in his rack, watched over by the savage gaze of the Iron Maiden rock band poster on his wall and drinking himself into a stupor.

Dahmer would mix a martini, or pop a dark German beer, slap in Black Sabbath's new hit *Heaven and Hell* tape, pull the headset down tight over his ears, and jack up the volume on "Neon Knights" and "Wall Away." Then he would lie back against the crisp, white pillow, shut his eyes, and get lost in the thunder of heavy metal.

Quite frankly, his fellow soldiers preferred for him to do his drinking flat on his back, his thoughts corralled by the throbbing music in his own little distant world. When Dahmer was not drinking, he was a good guy, amiable and able to joke around, doing his imitation of a wiseass drunk W. C. Fields for a few laughs. But with a snoot full of booze, he would lose what little control he might possess. Then his face would change into an angry mask and the pale eyes would just go empty, and the transformation would inevitably be followed by the shouts, the fights, the surliness, the arguments, and the eruptions of racist epithets. When drunk, Jeff Dahmer was a real pain in the ass. In a barracks filled with young soldiers of equal strength and training, the fights never developed beyond a bit of wrestling, but he was simply out of control when he was drunk. It was easier just to leave him alone.

That way he would be able to drink himself into black oblivion, sleep for a while, wake up, and do it all over again, passing out to either the blasting tunes of mainline metalers or the kill-your-daddy, fuck-your-mama, and butcher-your-cat lullabies howled by the coming new breed of head-knocking guitar bangers with tattoos of the devil on their arms.

Dahmer did his army time the way many soldiers did, passing through the Green Machine day by day until it was finally over. For Dahmer, however, the time also could be measured in bottles of beer and booze, and that habit brought his time to a quicker end than had been expected.

With his father at his side, he had signed up in the delayed-entry program four days after Christmas of 1978, took a bit of leave at his home in Bath before reporting, and finally went on active duty to start a three-year hitch on January 12, 1979. Dahmer was assigned to Fort McClellan, Alabama, because it was there that he could undergo the basic infantry training that all soldiers receive and then move immediately into advanced training for the line of work he had selected when he volunteered. The MOS, or military specialty, that he wanted was called 95-Bravo. That meant Jeff Dahmer wanted to be a military policeman, a person who could simultaneously help and be in control.

He did not make it through the rigorous MP program, however, and on May 11 he was transferred to Fort Sam Houston, outside of San Antonio, to endure the scalding heat of an early Texas summer until he completed training on June 22 as a medical specialist. During six weeks of intensive study, Dahmer learned the arts of the combat medic, a smorgasbord of talents that range from changing sheets on hospital beds to giving first aid to wounded soldiers, applying bandages and splints, doing whatever is necessary to keep them alive long enough to reach the doctors at an aid station in the rear. As part of his training, Dahmer received lectures in the anatomy of the human body, a knowledge that he would later put to grotesque use.

From Fort Sam, he was shipped off to West Germany, arriving at Baumholder a month later to become part of Headquarters Company in the Sixty-eighth Armored's Second Battalion. Baumholder is located about seventy miles southwest of Frankfurt, in the heart of the American military establishment in Germany. Most U.S. bases are clustered in the Rhineland-Palatinate state and are near the city of Kaiserslautern, better known to the GIs as K-Town, a place where years of American-German relations have left a somewhat mixed heritage of feelings. Things were not helped twenty years ago when an American soldier, who felt he was insulted in a K-Town bar, went back to his base and returned driving a U.S. Army tank. He squashed forty-six German cars and a mess of utility poles and other infrastructure items before being halted. The event is now part of German folklore and the people of K-Town tend to be wary of drunk American soldiers.

As a medic, Jeff Dahmer wore the uniform of

his country as part of a crack division of motorized infantry. He was backing up the crews of the Bradley fighting vehicles and other "tracks," as the treaded vehicles such as tanks and self-propelled guns are known, that are the steel teeth of a mech division.

But his drinking finally became more than just the usual dose of suds that any GI posted in Germany could be expected to absorb. The alcohol-induced wildness, the fights, the hangovers and the missed duty days finally got to him in his second year of service, as Dahmer lay abed, drinking. The army decided it might be better if PFC Dahmer departed for the civilian world back home. In a military unit, particulary one stationed in a potential hot spot, teamwork is essential and the soldiers need to be able to rely totally upon the men next to them. If one is a weak link, then he might be more suited to selling vacuum cleaners, or hustling tacos and burgers at a fast food joint, or working in a menial job at a chocolate factory. Among civilians, his mistakes would not get other people killed. The army decided to wash its hands of the problem soldier, giving him his walking papers after he refused to follow a program to tame his alcoholism.

There was no court-martial, but Dahmer was outprocessed at Fort Jackson, South Carolina, on March 26, 1981, two days after being shipped back from Germany. Instead of the full three-year hitch, he left the army after only two years, two months, and fifteen days. Although he was dismissed under the section of the Code of Military Justice that deals with alcohol and drug abuse, Dahmer has maintained that he was given an honorable discharge. Family members confirmed that his drinking problem was the reason he was dismissed from the service.

Years later, German police, alerted by the slayings in Milwaukee, would have questions about five unsolved murders that were committed in that country during the time PFC Dahmer was based in West Germany, protecting the frontiers of freedom. One of his army buddies would also say that perhaps Dahmer had been involved in the death of a German hitchhiker. But the accusations of overseas mayhem dimmed as Dahmer steadfastly insisted that he had never killed anyone in Germany.

That came as a great disappointment to the *Bild Zeitung*, the largest newspaper in the German-speaking world and one tilted more than slightly toward the sensational. The Hamburg-based tabloid, a creation of press lord Axel Springer, glories in gore. A recent article explained in great detail how a police sergeant and forest ranger in a Munich suburb answered a complaint about a barking dog. They found the animal, named Würstl (Little Sausage), hiding behind its owner but barking furiously. The officers thought Würstl looked threatening, so the cop hosed it down with three bursts from a submachine gun and the ranger administered the coup de grâce with his pistol. *Bild Zeitung* jumped on the Dahmer story like the cops on Würstl, running a front-page spread on Sunday, July 28, 1991, reporting to be the tale of someone who had encountered Dahmer while he was in the army. Its headline left absolutely nothing to the imagination. DAHMER WANTED TO CUT MY HEART OUT, it screeched.

But even taking into account the paper's sensationalist reputation, still the headline echoes strikingly the comment of an army buddy. Years later, after seeing photos of his old friend in the newspapers and reading the grisly accusations, the former soldier said that the news had left him shaken, realizing that when Dahmer had looked at him in that small barracks room, he might have been visualizing dinner.

And Dahmer's squad leader, with whom he had shared many hours, recalled what Jeff told him before leaving Germany on the fast track to a discharge for alcohol abuse. Dahmer said that he would be heard from again, sometime in the future, perhaps on television or in the newspapers.

CHAPTER SIX

Ein Prosit!

1981–1982

Lake Michigan, the only one of the five Great Lakes that lies wholly within the United States, hangs down like a limp finger pointing toward the section of the Midwest where industry ends and agriculture begins. The U.S.-Canadian border splits through Lakes Superior, Huron, Ontario, and Erie, leaving Lake Michigan as a wholly-owned entity that touches Wisconsin, Illinois, Indiana, and actually divides its namesake, the state of Michigan. At 321 miles long and 118 miles wide at its most distant points, this is not some little pond where one can stand on the shore and throw a stone across the water. Lake Michigan is one big piece of water.

It also was a navigable waterway all the way back to when Native Americans—or as they were called then, Indians—paddled their canoes along its sometimes placid, sometimes stormy coastline. To match its awesome size, it helped create awesome cities along its shores, the two largest of which are Chicago, near the southernmost point, and Milwaukee, on its western flank. The clear, fresh water of the lake would play an important part in the commercial development of what would become Milwaukee's most famous product.

From the start, Milwaukee was a meeting place. Even the earliest settlers, the Potawatomi Indians, referred to the site as the "Gathering Place by the Waters" and welcomed the first Europeans to trek the area, French explorers and traders coming down from the waterways of Canada in the 1630s. Some liked what they saw and established trading posts, bringing European-style commerce to the region, trading with the Indians for furs as the eighteenth century came to an end.

But French influence was destined to be relatively short, because within fifty years, the first wave of German immigrants flooded into the area, bringing with them their unique talent for brewing beer and cooking delicious food. The German dominance also would eventually fade, but its imprint stayed and influences Milwaukee to this day. To proclaim the city's friendliness, the residents of Milwaukee use the German term *gemütlich,* which as much reflects a style of life as an actual welcome.

The map of Wisconsin, a state with no mountains, is a checkerboard of towns and cities and villages called by foreign words, reflecting the comings and goings of throngs of different tribes, clans, nationalities, and races over the recent centuries. Indian names, such as Nekoosa and Black Hawk, French names like La Crosse and Eau Claire, and German ones like Berlin roll easily from the tongues of the Irish, Swedes, Hungarians, Serbs and Finns, African-Americans, Lao, and others who have found a home in Milwaukee. The city was a growth point located not too far east, not too far west, and painted in attractive colors for those envious and adventurous who wanted a slice of America in the early years, and a job with a paycheck in the more recent past. Oddly, while all of the other passersby have left a trail of names, the origin of the actual word "Milwaukee" has been lost in time. A passing religious man noted in his journal in 1679 that a tribe of Indians made their home at the mouth of the "Millioki River." That may have to do until scholars someday decide to figure it out.

At any rate, the flat place on the shore of Lake Michigan where the Menominee, the Kinnickinnic, and the Milwaukee rivers converge became a growing settlement, then officially a city in 1846, and eventually a modern metropolis that has a skyline of glittering office buildings, sophisticated dwellers, a beautiful waterfront and, as a German immigrant wrote, "streets as straight as a string."

Ownership of what was to become Wisconsin began in 1671 when it was formally claimed by the French, since the Indians had made the tragic mistake of not having a courthouse in which to write out a deed of their own. Almost a century later, Paris turned title over to London as part payment for losing the French and Indian War. The American Revolution came along twenty years later, and when it was over, the British ceded the lovely expanse of Wisconsin over to the colonials. Congress created the Wisconsin Territory in 1836, a dozen years before some politicians meeting in the town of Ripon created the Republican Party in the same year, 1848, that Wisconsin became the thirtieth state to join the Union.

The fact that Jeff Dahmer, an eccentric white man, could live without drawing much notice in a neighborhood predominantly populated by minorities reflects one of the unique elements of the personality of today's Milwaukee. The city has always prided itself on being a racial and cultural melting pot, a self-promoted image that residents believed until the Dahmer case showed it to be patently false.

But if that is not true, one thing that is absolutely certain is that if rubber made Akron, beer certainly made Milwaukee. Ironically, it was the armies of the Confederacy and a couple of Welsh-men who put the city firmly on track to becoming the beer capital of the United States. Milwaukee brews more beer than any other city, and its residents drink more beer per person than any other Americans.

Three immigrants from Wales put up the city's first brewery, tapping into, as have the brewers who followed, the cool, fresh waters of Lake Michigan and the hops grown by the farmers of Wisconsin. The early brewers, however, produced more whiskey and brandy than beer. Enter General Robert E. Lee, leading his secessionist forces into battle. Immediately, the northern states needed to raise money to equip troops to fight the Rebels, and a new dollar-per-barrel tax was passed on all alcoholic products. It did not take too long for the saloonkeepers to figure out that the financial return on the thirty-one gallons of beer that would fit in a barrel was better than on thirty-one gallons of brandy because customers ordered more glasses of beer. Milwaukee began drinking beer in great quantities, pushing up a need for more production and luring in new and more talented brewers.

The Germans came, bearing their rare talents from the old country, and soon successful breweries were founded that grew to giant companies such as Pabst, Schlitz, Blatz, and Miller. The big ones, as well as the small fry that fell by the competitive wayside—brands such as Little Willy Old Lager, Perplies, and Point Special—began making beer and money by the barrel from a thirsty America. It was said that an explorer found a bottle of Pabst at the North Pole, just one of the many advertising gimmicks that came along with the merry competition. With the money came political power, and the Germans had their day, at one time even requiring that the German language be taught to every schoolchild, from kindergarten on up.

Bars lined the streets and even industrial companies would hire a bucket boy to run out with a tray of empty jugs to the nearest saloon and fetch beer for the workers. When the mugs and glasses were raised aloft and "Ein Prosit!" rang out, it was more than a mere salute. It was a declaration of solidarity between a city and its product. When some legislator in Madison dared in the 1940s to say in a debate that alcoholic beverages might be as much of a scourge as illegal drugs, Assemblyman Leland S. McParland leaped to his feet to protest. "Whiskey? Why, whiskey is a food!"

To this city, where the cooking aroma of corn grits, ground malt, Lake Michigan water, and Wisconsin-grown hops permeates the air over some sections of town, where beer advertisements are everywhere and where even some fast-food stands have a keg on tap, was coming in 1982 an alcoholic young man named Jeffrey Dahmer. Dahmer, who everyone said was a terrible, fighting-mad drunk and who had been kicked out of the army for drinking, was coming home, back to the city of his birth, a German boy ready to drink his share of civic pride.

After being discharged from the army in South Carolina in March of 1981, Jeffrey slipped south into Florida, going all the way down to Miami and joining the legion of drifters soaking up the famous rays of the Sunshine State. After two years in Germany, it was good to be back in the United States, feeling the sunshine instead of the chill of central Europe, hearing the American voices on the street, checking out the tanned chicks in their bright swimsuits and chowing down on Cuban black beans and red rice. He found work slapping sandwiches together at a fast-food joint over the causeway in Miami Beach, and there was a brief chance that Dahmer might use the respite from his past to start anew in that golden summer. Once he found the bars, that hope perished in an alcoholic haze.

Shari and Lionel Dahmer kept track of him from their new place in Granger Township, Ohio, a nice townhouse in Medina County, right next door to Bath Township, but considerably more rural. They persuaded Jeffrey to come back to Ohio and he eventually agreed. But this was not an innocent boy any longer. He had killed a man with his bare hands, he had been through the army, he had walked the streets of K-Town in Germany, and he had drifted on the Gold Coast of Florida. Granger Township, for all of its attractions, was just too small.

He fell back into the old habits that his father remembered so well, mainly going out and getting drunk, staying at bars until closing time, demanding more to drink even though he was unable to remember where he'd left the family car, and eventually getting into fights; he'd end up getting decked by someone and sobering up with a few new bruises and another ounce of hatred. On October 7, 1981, he carried his open bottle of vodka into the lounge of the Ramada Inn in Bath, arrogant and drunk. He refused to leave and tussled with the police when they came. They arrested him for disorderly conduct, resisting arrest, and carrying an open container of liquor. Sixty dollars, said the magistrate, who suspended an accompanying ten-day sentence in the slammer.

It was decided that the tranquil surroundings were not sufficiently beneficial and that perhaps living in the house in West Allis, Wisconsin, close to his grandmother, might make a difference.

South of Milwaukee, beside Interstate 94, is the sprawl of Mitchell Field, the city's major airport. It was named to honor General William Mitchell, the aviation pioneer who proved that airplanes could sink battleships and forever changed the face of aerial warfare, although that did not save him from a court-martial. As a boy, Mitchell played on a huge expanse of lawn in the nearby town of West Allis, where his family owned an immense estate called Meadowmere. That fact is noted on a plaque erected by the West Allis Rotary Club in a tiny triangle of grass where Hayes Avenue splits around a leafy island of trees at the end of the 2300 block of South Fifty-seventh Street in West Allis, a place where another Milwaukee native was about to make a name for himself.

The community has evolved over the years into a charmingly well-kept little village on the flank of Milwaukee. Lawns are mowed, sidewalks are swept, and cleanliness seems to be a dominant theme, proven by the condition of the paved alleyways behind the homes. It is what urban planners would call a nice place to live.

One of those immaculate little homes, a two-story doll house, white siding over tan block and with red shutters on the three top front windows, belongs to Catherine Dahmer, the paternal grandmother of Jeffrey and the person to whom he felt the closest. The home has a trellis of purple flowers growing beside a side door reached by a half-circle of a walkway, a private entrance that leads to a downstairs apartment. In the backyard, well-tended beds of flowers thrive in the crisp Wisconsin air, giving a summerlong burst of color to the neat neighborhood.

Jeffrey, exiled from the army and rootless after staying with his father and stepmother, readily agreed to return to the home of his grandmother. Catherine, although in her seventies, gave her grandson a warm hug and a key to the door. It was thought that with some stability and a base in a friendly and familiar environment, Jeffrey might settle down, ease off on his drinking, and finally begin to mature. A comfortable bed in a place he knew well and the rust-colored, shingled roof over his head might provide the security that he sought.

Indeed, when Jeffrey was around his grandmother, he puttered with her in the garden, planting roses and keeping the lawn mowed to match all the other neat plots of grass on South Fifth-seventh Street. Using the medic's skills he had learned in the army, he found work drawing blood at Milwaukee Blood Plasma, Inc., and for a time things were looking up. As usual, though, a black thundercloud of misfortune hovered just around the corner, waiting for him.

He was laid off of the blood bank job in 1982, and in August, when the Wisconsin State Fair rolled into town and farmers from around the state hauled in huge blocks of cheese for a grading competition, Jeffrey was arrested again. Police reported that he had exposed himself, charged him with indecent exposure, and slapped him with another fine.

It would not be long before his taste for blood would surface again.

CHAPTER SEVEN

Three Cops

Monday, May 27, 1991

Between them, Officers John Balcerzak, Joseph Gabrish, and Richard Porubcan had sixteen years of police work and a stack of citations for meritorious service when they entered the Oxford Apartments in the early hours of that Memorial Day Monday, trying to figure out what was happening between the big white guy and the zonked Asian male. They knew that any number of things might happen as a result of whatever decision they made in such a field investigation, for in any dispute, someone would be unhappy and might complain to higher levels of the Police Department. But they had no idea whatsoever that they were about to unleash a whirlwind that would rock their employer, the city of Milwaukee, to its foundations.

They coaxed the two males who were the center of the disturbance through the wooden door of apartment 213 and stepped into a rectangular room that was a combined kitchen, dining area, and living room. At the far end was a sliding window, the curtains partially open, and in the right-hand corner an aquarium containing a couple of fish sat on a small table beneath some sort of horn hanging by a strap. Between the aquarium and the open door was a sofa, and beside it an end table littered with beer cans and cigarette butts in an ashtray. The door would swing open until it bumped into a combination refrigerator-freezer that stood beside a sink and four-burner stove. The side wall was taken up with a dining table and two chairs and a squat, floor-standing freezer. The sliding door to the bedroom and the bath area was closed. In other words, they saw a typical one-bedroom apartment, one that was unusually tidy for being the residence of a single male. A couple of power tools lay on the living room carpet. Polaroid photographs of men in various stages of undress were strewn about, and the Asian's clothes lay on the couch.

Dahmer had provided a piece of identification that had his picture on it, so the officers knew who he was, and when they got into the apartment, he handed them some Polaroids of the younger guy, who was pictured wearing only some briefs. A union lawyer would eventually report that while the interview was being conducted, the Asian sat quietly on the sofa, making no attempt to flee nor raise a ruckus about his treatment.

The emergency medical technicians that had arrived had determined that there were no serious injuries involved, and Dahmer was calm and cool in talking with the officers, very persuasive in his spiel that the incident was nothing but a disagreement between himself and his gay boyfriend. He said that the Asian was nineteen years old, which meant he was an adult—and adults could do what they damned well please behind closed doors.

So it came down to a decision that would be based upon the experience gleaned by the three cops over the years. According to a copyrighted story in the *Milwaukee Journal*, Balcerzak had been wearing a shield for six years, Gabrish had begun police work by doing the dirty-fingernail clerical duties of an aide in 1982, and Porubcan, the youngest of the three, was a computer fanatic fresh out of the academy, class of 1990, and already credited with five merit arrests while still in his probationary stage. Balcerzak and Gabrish had qualified to be field training officers who could guide rookies through the minefields of law enforcement out on the streets, where things can look different during a midnight frontline confrontation than they do under the glare of fluorescent lights in an office somewhere, when men and women in civilian office garb comb through your reports for mistakes before they go to lunch. The three had a reputation among their fellow street patrolmen. They were good cops.

And in this case, they saw nothing to indicate that foul play had either taken place or was about to. Like many people before them, they were bamboozled by the courteous Dr. Jekyll side of Jeffrey Dahmer's personality. The Mr. Hyde part, after having had many run-ins with the police, now hid somewhere deep inside Dahmer when badges came on the scene.

A veteran of the Milwaukee department who wished to remain anonymous spelled it out. There had been a complaint, and it had been answered. One guy is barely able to speak, but not trying to run away. The other guy is apparently sober enough to explain the situation and has pictures that indicate a homosexual relationship may be involved. Okay, so what's your call?

The three officers made the mistake of their lifetime. They believed the story put forth by Jeffrey Dahmer and they walked away, leaving Konerak Sinthasomphone to his horrible fate. Then they compounded the error, probably committing professional suicide in the process, by joking around when they called into the District Three station house on West Vliet Street. They laughed about the boyfriends they had just encountered, and the uncaring tape recorder caught it all. The conversation would be played a thousand times in a thousand cities when the case exploded in the headlines.

In two months, after the extent of Jeffrey Dahmer's butchery became known to the world, things happened fast, particularly when Glenda Cleveland let it be known that police had been called to that slaughterhouse and had walked away. Five people would be murdered there between the time the three officers left and the day Dahmer's butchery would finally be brought to a halt.

While the nation was astounded by the mass slaughter, Milwaukee's minority population was furious. They wanted to know if it was a tragic case of racial discrimination, if the white policemen had given Jeffrey Dahmer easier treatment because he was white while his victim was Laotian, a brother of colored skin. It was a question that would rattle Milwaukee for months.

In answer to the rising chorus of protest, Police Chief Philip Arreola suspended the three policemen pending an investigation, and later filed adminstrative charges against them for failing to conduct a proper investigation. Mayor John Norquist said he would not prejudge the officers, but that he was outraged by what had happened. Suddenly, the Dahmer situation was more than a murder case, it was a morality play with a heavy dose of politics involved, and a demoralized police force hit the streets to deal with minority residents who had found still another reason not to trust them.

CHAPTER EIGHT

Grandma's House

January 14, 1985–September 25, 1988

Something good was in the air for Jeffrey Dahmer. To be precise, it was the combined sweet smell of money and chocolate. He had been out of steady work since being laid off at the blood bank more than two years earlier, but with his grandmother providing the essentials of food and lodging, he had been able to squeak through the economic hard times. Now, help was at hand in the big, square, industrial-style building at Fifth Street and Highland Avenue on the flank of downtown Milwaukee.

The Ambrosia Chocolate Company exudes a pleasant odor of cooking chocolate that sometimes clashes in the noses of passersby with the beer-brewing smell coming from the big Pabst plant a few blocks away at Juneau and Ninth. Inside the little retail shop that is tucked into the side of the block-long building, chocolate of all shapes is for sale from barrels, shelves, bins, and counters. A bright sign on the far wall declares that Ambrosia produces the "Food of the Gods." Jeffrey Dahmer, who had so little luck holding on to anything in his life, got a job on January 14, 1985, as a laborer at the Ambrosia Chocolate Company, drawing a paycheck of $8.25 per hour. He would hold the job for six years, an extraordinary slice of stability in a life that was careering out of control. His job would last until just before he was arrested for the final time. Meanwhile, he would learn how to mix chocolate. Vats of it.

The steady paycheck and the overnight shift from 11:00 P.M. until 7:30 A.M., when he could work with fewer supervisors around and not be required to have contact with the public, appealed to Dahmer and things began to come under control in at least part of his life. Even so, when he was not at work, he was still a loose cannon.

He had no close friends, didn't really trust people, and had never had a decent relationship with a woman. But with a good-paying job, he even allowed himself to think that someday, marriage might be a possibility, according to later probation reports. That was simply a false euphoria, for Jeffrey was already discovering that he was gay and that he could receive sexual gratification from other men, something he would not openly admit until 1991, when he began to discuss it during probation interviews. And when he reflected upon his sexual preferences, he figured that he had begun feeling homosexual tendencies as far back as high school. The gay life-style around Milwaukee was very attractive to him because not much was asked by one partner of another when both had generally accepted the idea of a one-night stand.

He began to frequent the hangouts of the male homosexual community and frequently convinced his unsuspecting companions to drink a concoction that he was perfecting, a potion that would make them pass out, rendering them unconscious and totally under his control. One of his laboratories was the Club Bath Milwaukee, where he experimented with various patrons over a period of several months. Clad only in a towel, he would flirt with another man, lure him back to a private cubicle, and pour him a drink. Like any experiment, there was trial and error, some of the men not responding at all, while others got sick and at least one ended up in the hospital. Some who recalled the incidents later would say that Dahmer did not seem to care whether he could have sex with them, just whether they would take the drink. After paramedics and police showed up one night to talk to the customers when a drugged patron was too long in waking up, the management of Club Bath Milwaukee in 1986 told Jeffrey Dahmer to go away and never come back. He was bad news and the club was off limits to him. The bathhouse was closed two years later by the city. His family reported that his grandmother once went downstairs unannounced and discovered Jeffrey there with a young black man, who seemed drunk. As she watched, the black man fell down and hit his head. A shaken Catherine Dahmer went back upstairs.

The eventual full expression of Dahmer's gay life-style was still in the future, but his exhibitionist tendency was about to land him in serious trouble for the first time.

In his own words, as told to a probation officer, this is what happened on September 8, 1986, on a grassy slope beside the Kinnickinnic River: "I was drinking some beer in an undeveloped wooded area alone. After a few cans of beer I needed to go, so I did, behind some trees. I was sure there was no one else around, but I was wrong. Two boys saw me and called the police."

That's not what the two boys, both twelve years old, said. They told police that Dahmer's pants and undershorts had been pulled down and he was standing in clear view. Jeffrey was masturbating. He had chosen to flash little boys, not little girls, and told the cop who booked him for lewd and lascivious behavior that he had done it before, a story that he would later change and stick to as if he were reciting gospel.

On March 10, 1987, a Milwaukee County Circuit Court convicted Jeffrey Dahmer of the reduced charge of disorderly conduct and Judge Arlene Connors gave him a suspended one-year sentence, ordered him to undergo a complete course of counseling, and handed him a bill for forty-two dollars in court costs. His grandmother, with whom he was still living, was unaware of the offense.

"I'll never go back in the woods again," he told the probation officers, insisting that he had no idea that the two kids had seen him. He also confided that he had been "put through the wringer" by some policemen on an unspecified earlier encounter for shoplifting a coat back when he didn't have a job. And he admitted that he was slugging back a twelve-pack of beer on the weekends, "sometimes."

Throughout 1987 Dahmer stayed in contact with the probation officers, coming in personally or giving them a telephone call. In a pattern that would be repeated for years, the officers themselves never went to see him, staying deskbound rather than personally investigating his living arrangements. He went through the questionnaires that were thrust at him, did the mandatory reporting, but soon tired of the psychological counseling sessions that had been arranged, continuing them only because the court had ordered him to do so. He was on a very loose and long leash. On a positive note, he received a pay raise at work, going to $8.50 an hour, quite a bit of money for a young person who lived in his grandmother's house. It meant that he had money jingling in his pockets when he went out to cruise the bars, money he could flash to buy a favor here and there.

On September 9, 1987, Dahmer came to the probation office and filled out the required monthly report, saying that he had not changed his address, borrowed any money, had any contacts with the police, changed his job, or bought an automobile since he had filled out his last monthly report on August 12, which was his last monthly session. In his sharply right-tilting handwriting, he signed it at the bottom. A scribbled note by an official, on an accompanying piece of paper, indicates Dahmer did not see a probation agent that day. Dahmer's reports for September and October were as clean as a whistle, except to note that Jeffrey missed one day of work in October because he was sick.

Six days after walking out of the probation office door on September 9, Jeffrey Dahmer would kill again.

Steven W. Tuomi was a twenty-four-year-old man who had drifted to Milwaukee from his hometown of Ontonagon, Michigan, a tiny community of only about twenty-four hundred people on the bleak shore of Lake Superior. Almost at the western tip of Michigan's Upper Peninsula, Ontonagon is midway between the Fire Steel River and the Porcupine Mountains. A young man might eschew the natural beauty of the place in favor of something a bit more exciting, like living in a big city, a city like Milwaukee.

Tuomi was one such person, although the life that he lived in Milwaukee was hardly of the style that he would be able to brag about to his chums back in Ontonagon. He found work as a short-order cook and took lodgings at a place on the lower east side of Milwaukee, on Cass Street.

On September 15, his path crossed that of Jeffrey Dahmer, a tall, kind of good-looking guy with a self-deprecating sense of humor. Dahmer later would be unable to give too many details of what happened that night, other than that the two of them ended up going back to his apartment in West Allis. The result was grim, because Steve Tuomi was rewarded for befriending Dahmer by being killed, then butchered like a cow. He was never seen again, and his family, worried about the lack of contact, officially reported him missing in December 1987.

For Dahmer, killing was becoming easier. At least nine long years had elapsed between the murder of Steve Hicks in 1978 and the day Tuomi fell under his knife. The pace between victims soon would be measured in months, and finally in mere days and sometimes only in hours.

Bodies. When he killed Steve Hicks, Dahmer had had some logistical problems disposing of the remains, but he'd solved those by getting rid of the flesh and scattering the fragmented bones. But that was in rural Ohio, not in a neighborhood where houses and people were all around. He had to come up with a plan of action.

His solution was a gory one.

Catherine Dahmer complained to Lionel and Shari Dahmer about some of the goings-on at her house, particularly about the bad smell in the garage, a sticky smell that would linger even though the garbage had long been picked up. Upon coming over to West Allis and making a personal investigation, Lionel Dahmer discovered that the garage had some sort of odoriferous residue in it, something black and slimy. He questioned his son.

Jeffrey told his father that he had been conducting some experiments in which he used chemicals to melt down the flesh and fur of dead animals he had found—sort of like what he had done with the childhood chemistry set that had been a present from his parents. His father, a respected and highly trained chemist, knew exactly what acids could and could not do. He thought that his son might have a screw loose and told him so to his face. What Jeffrey was doing was more than gruesome, it was downright strange and weird, the father said. But like all parents who want to believe the best possible scenarios, he bought the whole story.

Meanwhile, Jeffrey had solved his problems. He was using a vat of acid to strip the flesh from the bones, then throwing the whole mess away. Except for a few keepsakes.

Time began to pass quickly. The nation's attention was focused on Washington, where Lieutenant Colonel Oliver North was explaining his role in the Iran-Contra scandal. Around the country, candidates of every stripe were tossing their hats into the ring for the 1988 presidential election. In Milwaukee, Jeffrey Dahmer was becoming very good at what he was doing and was preparing to do it again.

In January of 1988, Dahmer picked up a four-teen-year-old native Americn boy on a street corner, took him to the basement flat in West Allis, and killed him there. He would not be identified until well after Dahmer was arrested.

Dahmer filed the usual probation report on March 10, saying he had missed a day of mixing chocolate because he was sick. It was the last time he'd be required to report in because of the disorderly conduct charge. On March 20, 1988, the Division of Corrections, Department of Health and Social Services, State of Wisconsin declared that "Jeffrey Dahmer has satisfied all conditions of said (one year) probation" and that, retroactive ten days, he was "discharged absolutely." No one was looking over his shoulder anymore.

Richard Guerrero was a good-looking guy, short and slender, with dark eyes and a slightly unruly head of thick, black hair. On March 24, 1988, he walked out of his parents' home on the north side of Milwaukee, wearing a coat to ward off the chilly weather. He said he was going over to see a friend. The friend said Richard never arrived.

Jeffrey Dahmer, four days after being discharged from probation, locked his hazel eyes on the young man, who was only twenty-one years old and the youngest of six children. Since Richard didn't have a job, he had left the house with only three bucks and no wallet. That would have made him an easy target for someone who bought him a drink and perhaps offered money to pose for a few pictures. Guerrero was lured back to the Meadowmere area of West Allis. Standing only five foot six and weighing 130 pounds, a graceful kid who liked to dance, he would be no match for the six-foot Dahmer, who weighed about 175. He wasn't. Richard Guerrero became Victim Number Four.

By September, Catherine Dahmer had finally reached the end of her patience with Jeffrey. Grandson or not, she was getting too old to put up with the foolishness going on down in the basement, the noises and the chemical smells. She preferred to live alone, she told the family. Jeffrey had to go.

Once again, he was being abandoned. In his view, even his grandmother, although she would go out of her way in future years to stay in touch with him, did not want him around. The fact that he pushed people who loved him far beyond their limits of tolerance did not seem to occur to him.

On September 25, Jeffrey obeyed. He packed up his things and moved. He had found a cheap place in a rundown neighborhood not far from Marquette University, a one-bedroom rental flat in the boxy, white Oxford Apartments at 924 North Twenty-fifth Street. There, he would almost immediately launch onto a path of destruction, a nightmare killing spree that would eventually horrify the nation.

CHAPTER NINE

"The World Has Enough Misery . . ."

September 26, 1988

It was as though he had crossed a bridge. At one end of the span was the place he was leaving, the places in which he had grown up among the well-groomed yards and tranquil settings of Bath Township and West Allis, where people lived the dreams of middle-class America. Everyone had cars, VCRs, credit cards, and a future. At the other end of the bridge lay the quagmire of the disenfranchised, the underclass of people who hadn't quite made it far enough up the social ladder to escape the stubborn pull of despair. The main thing on a person's mind at the far end of the bridge was from where the next meal and the month's rent money would come. Hope could be a cruel joke on the meaner side of town. In such a place, you mind your own business, for that is a big enough task by itself on any given day. Jeffrey Dahmer found himself in a situation like the one in the childhood fable of Br'er Rabbit, who escaped a tight spot by getting himself heaved into a briar patch. As a rabbit thrives in a thicket of stickers, and a shark thrives in a busy ocean, Dahmer would soon discover that on the near west side of Milwaukee, he could get away with murder.

There are several Milwaukees that can be viewed as the city spreads out to the west, away from one of the most beautiful waterfront areas in America. While Boston harbor may be stifled with pollution and in coastal Long Beach, California, the raindrops are sometimes coated with oil, the lakefront area of Milwaukee has been carefully tended over the years and is the ideal dwelling place for the monied. Green trees seem to march over grassy slopes toward the water, and out toward the flatline horizon of Lake Michigan, the triangular white sails of cruising pleasure boats stand out like banners for the good life. Genteel mansions rest in lines of quiet dignity along Lake Drive, and high-rises, condominiums, and town homes spread north toward Whitefish Bay and Fox Point. This is a fine place in which to live.

Not all of Milwaukee is like that. One of those straight-as-string streets for which the city is known is Wisconsin Avenue, a thoroughfare that heads west, not north, anchored at one end by the thriving and prosperous downtown area. Huge new buildings, renovated shopping districts, exciting entertainment, and places to make big bucks are all downtown, where men in Italian suits and women in silk can power-graze with the best of them. It isn't New York or San Francisco or Dallas, but the life-style downtown can be rewarding.

From that mercantile oasis, Wisconsin Avenue threads its way west and divides the campus of Marquette University, where Lionel Dahmer once went to school and where students in the latest L.L. Bean and Banana Republic slacks and sweaters study in the cloistered halls of a Jesuit-run university. Just beyond Marquette, when Wisconsin Avenue leaves behind the streets that end with "teen" and enters the twenties, things change quickly. Once the very wealthy lived in this area, too, as evidenced by the rococo mansion of Frederick Pabst that still stands in isolated splendor, open to tourists every day. But these days, the area is a belt of lower-income neighborhoods where crime is high, drugs are abundant, and people get by one day at a time. Wisconsin Avenue continues its westward trek and soon finds its way into more refined neighborhoods, but the residents of the near west side normally don't ride the white-and-green buses of the Milwaukee

Transportation Authority much beyond North Twenty-seventh. And the residents of the ritzy flats in North Point won't often be found walking a poodle around there late at night.

And while it would be discovered that Dahmer could get away with murder in this place, he couldn't get away with molesting a teenage Laotian boy. At least, not the first time he tried.

Dahmer moved into a second-floor flat, apartment number 213, at 924 North Twenty-fifth Street on September 25, 1988, and the very next day decided to try out some old habits in his new place. Only a few months out of a probationary period for exposing himself to small boys, he gave in to his pedophilic craving once again.

He met a young Asian boy out on the street near his apartment complex and offered him fifty dollars if the kid would pose for some photographs. Dahmer said he wanted to try out a new camera he had purchased. The boy was only thirteen years of age, one of the children of a Laotian family named Sinthasomphone that lived nearby.

Once inside his apartment, Dahmer coaxed the child into drinking a cup of coffee into which he had poured some liquid. Then he had him drink even more of the sedative-laced coffee. The youngster began to feel disoriented and woozy as Dahmer moved close and began to fondle the boy's genitals. Dahmer whispered to the boy that he wanted him to look sexier in the photographs.

In an amazing feat, something that Jeffrey Dahmer would rarely allow to happen, the dazed teenager staggered to the door and outside, stumbling safely home. The family took their son to the hospital and the police were notified. Officers paid their first visit to the Oxford Apartments to see Jeffrey Dahmer.

Dahmer was arrested and charged with second-degree sexual assault and enticing a child for immoral purposes. What followed in the trial would be examined minutely in coming years. But things that seem clear now were invisible then, even to the experts whose job it was to determine the status of such things.

A week after his arrest, Dahmer was released from custody on bail, going back to his apartment, his job, and the streets, while both the state and Gerald Boyle, the lawyer hired to defend Dahmer, put together their cases. Case Number F88-2515 began working its way through the Milwaukee County Circuit Court system and the trial before Judge William D. Gardner was set for May 1989.

That was too bad for Anthony Sears.

Anthony Sears was a friendly, nice-looking young man who had thoughts about someday becoming a model, but at the time he was quite satisfied with his new job as manager of a Baker's Square restaurant. Certainly he was not shy when a camera was pointed his way, flashing a big smile and fixing his dark eyes directly on the lens. His unblemished, oval face was framed by thick black hair that was full at the sides and reached below his collar in back. He had given no indication to either his mother or his girlfriend that anything might be troubling him, other than his wish to eventually leave Milwaukee. His face would bring him fame and fortune if he could find the right situation, he felt.

On March 25, 1989, just before Jeffrey Dahmer was to go on trial, Sears and a friend went out drinking at LaCage, a bar on Second Street and National that was popular with the homosexual community.

The old two-story building has a rather aged top floor of gray brick and white wood, and the lower exterior is painted in a faded dark red. There is no sign outside the bar, so strangers do not frequent the place. This is not an uptown fern bar, but actually a saloon in a dilapidated area of similar bars and saloons, down the street from the Hispanic center of the city. Perhaps the most symbolic part of the block is not the bars that come and go, but the old fire station that housed Engine Company Number 3. Once a point of community energy, the old stone building is now shuttered and closed, a victim of the times.

But right next door, once a patron is inside LaCage, things tend to jump. Music, TV, conversation, drinks, and good times. It's a place to meet new friends. A tall white man named Jeff, who said that he was in Milwaukee from Chicago to visit his grandmother, struck up a conversation with handsome Anthony Sears and his friend. They all hung around drinking until the bar finally closed, when Dahmer made his pitch and Sears caught it. Drinks, photographs, love into the early-morning hours. To others in La-Cage that night, Anthony Sears was a neat guy. To the man buying him drinks, he looked like Victim Number Five.

They persuaded the friend, who had a car, to give them a ride over to West Allis, where Dahmer said his grandmother lived at Lincoln and Fifty-sixth. It was the sort of lie he would repeat later, giving a false address to anyone accompanying a victim. They piled into the car and drove over, with Dahmer and Sears getting out at the intersection that was just north of his grandmother's house. The friend drove away, leaving the two young men alone, potential lovers headed for an assignation. He did not know an exact address that might have been of interest to the police later on.

Dahmer did not use his own flat for this meeting but had returned to West Allis, perhaps because he was worried that the police might be keeping an eye on the Oxford Apartments.

At his grandmother's house, they went through the white side door and down the stairs, and when they reached the little flat, according to police records, they engaged in sex, then Dahmer poured Sears a drink heavily laced with his homemade brew of sleeping potion. The pleasant evening ended and the madness began as Jeffrey changed again, his eyes going flat and his face contorting in response to the messages from his private, inner hell.

With Sears drunk and disabled, Dahmer strangled him. Then he began the awful chore of chop-
ping the body to pieces. It has been assumed that
he simply threw the body parts away with the
trash, something that he would do repeatedly
before his crime spree was over. He finished the
job by boiling the decapitated head of his recent
lover until the skin peeled off. When the skull
was cleaned, he painted it gray. When he finally
went back to his apartment on Twenty-fifth
Street, he took a souvenir with him. The painted
skull of Anthony Sears would eventually be found
by police in Dahmer's apartment.

Jeffrey Dahmer walked into court in May with
five deaths on his hands, but facing the law only
for molesting a Laotian teenager. Transcripts indicate that the prosecution wanted the judge to
throw the book at the defendant.

On May 23, at a sentencing hearing, Assistant
District Attorney Gale Shelton declared that the
record of his past infractions showed that Dahmer had no intention of mending his ways, that
the only treatment he would accept probably
would have to come within the justice system. She
wanted him jailed for at least five years, followed
by strict probation.

The testimony, Shelton said, had shown that
Dahmer felt the only thing he had done wrong in
this instance was to pick up a boy who was underage. She contended he knew perfectly well that
the quiet boy he was toying with on his sofa was
not an adult. To her, it was a miracle that the

child had escaped safely. And, with considerable insight, she said the defendant had at least one special talent. He was very manipulative, able to show the appropriate reactions to authority while still boiling inside.

How manipulative was he? Gerald Boyle, his lawyer, would find out later that he didn't have a clue about what his client was really up to, despite all of the pretrial work. Boyle told Judge Gardner that the truth of the matter was that Jeffrey Dahmer had stumbled badly this one time, but since being arrested the previous September, he had kept his record clean, despite not having undergone treatment for his alcoholism. He went to work at the chocolate factory every night without incident and, in Boyle's opinion, the police nailing him on this charge probably had headed off further trouble. Give him a long sentence with no jail time but plenty of probational supervision, the lawyer told the court. Lionel Dahmer also addressed Gardner and said his boy needed help, professional treatment, not a crippling term in prison.

Then Jeffrey Dahmer got to talk, and he put on his sackcloth-and-ashes routine. He said the experience of being arrested and brought up on charges had been a living nightmare for him; it was enough of a shock to make him mend his ways. He said he knew he was an alcoholic and a homosexual, and was terribly sorry that he had picked up a young boy. But now he was ready to turn his life around, work hard, and become a productive member of society.

The judge expressed his own concern, particularly that the prison system of Wisconsin did not have a treatment program for its inmates with alcohol and sexual problems. If Dahmer went in to do hard time, he probably would come out worse than he already was, the judge felt. He said the type of crime was severe enough that a judge might take the prosecutor's plea to heart and wave goodbye to the defendant for twenty years. But the jurist wanted a chance to salvage Jeffrey Dahmer and therefore made his choice: Jeffrey Dahmer was found guilty of second-degree sexual assault and enticing a child for immoral purposes and was sentenced on May 24 to three years in prison, a term that was reduced to one year on a work-release program, followed by five years of probation and "in-patient or out-patient alcohol treatment." He was prohibited by the court from having contact with anyone under the age of eighteen.

Assistant D.A. Shelton had warned them all. Once he was out of prison Dahmer probably would commit more crimes, she predicted. It was a perfectly accurate statement.

So Jeffrey Dahmer walked away from another collision with the law, sentenced to a year on a loose program for molestation, but not spending a day, not an hour, not a minute behind bars for killing five people.

Meanwhile, his victim was shattered by the

experience. Despite being part of a close-knit Asian family, the boy withdrew into himself whenever the incident was mentioned. Years later, he would not discuss it, even with his brothers.

Although sentenced to do his time at the House of Correction in Franklin, southwest of the city, Dahmer was shifted to the Community Correctional Center at 1004 North Tenth Street, right smack in the middle of downtown Milwaukee, for convenience. By walking a block toward the water and crossing Highland, he was at the door of the Ambrosia Chocolate Company in time for work each night, getting paid almost $9.00 per hour for a job that he had held for five years. He would return to his cell in the morning and go to sleep. He was only fifteen blocks from his apartment.

Not necessarily a model prisoner, Dahmer learned how the game was played, saying and doing the right things to win "good time" that would subtract days from his sentence for not making trouble. He was quiet, but he couldn't turn off his churning brain. He once confided to a fellow inmate that he hated black people and would like to kill a thousand of them. A guy who mixed chocolates on the overnight shift wanted to kill people. Sure. The other guy laughed at the idea.

Thanksgiving of 1989 came and the family gathered at Catherine Dahmer's home in West Allis. Jeffrey was given a twelve-hour pass for the special occasion. He was late reporting back to the correctional center and reeked of alcohol when he came close to a guard. When he failed a balloon test for sobriety, Tennessee sipping whiskey cost him two days of good time. Inmates at the CCC said Dahmer never went to his grandmother's house for Thanksgiving turkey, choosing instead to go somewhere and knock back a quart of Jack Daniel's bourbon.

Oblivious to the irony, only a few days later, on December 10, Dahmer once again tried to con the judge. He sent Gardner an extraordinary, handprinted note pleading for leniency. The man who had already killed without mercy on numerous occasions, molested a thirteen-year-old boy, exposed himself to two twelve-year-old boys, and had a turbulent history with alcohol pleaded with the jurist to give him a break.

The 29-line correspondence started out by reviewing his case and noting that he had entered a guilty plea, but he said he was charged with taking photographs of a 13-year-old boy, and did not mention the actual charges, which were the much more serious crimes of sexual assault and enticing a child for immoral purposes.

He told the judge that he pled guilty because he felt that a man should accept responsibility for his mistakes. He wrote that during his incarceration in the work-release program, he had had an opportunity to examine his life from a new perspective that he had never encountered before and Dahmer labeled his actions as being shameful. In an extraordinarily prescient statement, Dahmer then stated that, in his opinion, there was enough suffering in the world without him contributing more.

Then he promised the judge that he would never let such an event take place again, and he requested that the judge modify, meaning reduce, the sentence. That way, Dahmer wrote, he could resume his life and live it as a productive member of society.

He was to eventually serve ten months of his one-year sentence, but before Jeffrey was released, another letter was written to Gardner, this one from Lionel Dahmer, the defendant's beleaguered father.

On March 1, 1990, Lionel made his most forceful attempt to date to alter the destructive path that his eldest son was taking. He wrote Gardner a heart-wrenching letter pleading for Jeffrey to be forced to undergo treatment for alcoholism and expressing "tremendous reservations" about what would happen if professional help was not ordered.

Lionel expressed concern that Jeffrey was not receiving the alcoholism treatment that the judge had instructed Jeffrey be given during his sentence.

The elder Dahmer said he was concerned that if Jeffrey were released from jail without undergoing some rehabilitative treatment, his son might fall prey to the same influences that had led him into trouble in the first place. He was specifically addressing Jeffrey's drinking problem and said that a psychologist Jeffrey had seen after the conviction for indecent exposure had not been an alcoholism specialist and that no substantive reports on his alcoholism were being given to the court or the probationary officials.

Lionel Dahmer wrote that since no alcoholism treatment was being pursued, he had serious concerns about how Jeff would fare when released.

He said that every problem that had marred his son's life could be traced directly to alcohol abuse and asked the jurist to actively intervene and, if necessary, force Jeffrey to undergo treatment. Dahmer's concern showed through plainly in his closing sentence, in which he said the moment at hand might represent the final opportunity to successfully curb Jeffrey's drinking problem.

On March 2, the day after Lionel posted the letter to the court, Jeffrey Dahmer walked out of the CCC, once again a free man.

There wasn't a ripple in the community. Milwaukee was not in the grip of shock nor in a state of terror. No one knew a mass murderer had been behind bars and was now back on the streets. A very ordinary man, tall, slim, and with blond hair and empty eyes, was strolling the streets, under instruction to meet with his probation officer, Donna Chester, at least every other week.

In the meanwhile, Chester told Dahmer, he was to have no unsupervised contact with anyone under the age of eighteen without prior permission from his parole agent; he was not to do any illegal drugs whatsoever; he was to take part in substance abuse treatment; he was to undergo some psychotherapy, including on the sexuality issue; he was not to contact the boy that he had molested; and "you shall consume no alcohol whatsoever."

The words looked good on paper, but were worthless before the ink was dry.

CHAPTER TEN

Rampage

June 14, 1990—December 1990

The bloodletting erupted anew for a year and a month. Dahmer slew a dozen men within that span of thirteen months, charming victims from out of town, from the gay bars, picking them up at bus stops, shopping centers, and straight off the street. The only pattern to the killings was that they were as random as could be, an ordinary man doing extraordinary things. It was only when the dying time came that Dahmer would lapse into the familiar routine of drugging the victim, strangling them, taking pictures, dismembering their bodies, taking more pictures, and stashing skulls and body parts all over his apartment. At one point, he later told police questioners, he felt he was getting better at cutting up the corpses. But he was spinning further out of control all the time. Killing them wasn't enough. He introduced some awful new wrinkles. Such as necrophilia, having sex with the body of a freshly slain person. And, he would claim later, putting away parts of bodies to eat later. Cannibalism.

No one in Milwaukee even knew that a serial killer was on the loose. When Dahmer finally was stopped, it was because one of his potential victims had slipped from his grasp, not because of a telephone call from a witness or a neighbor, not because of the watchful eye of the state's probation officers, and certainly not because of any sleuthing by the Milwaukee Police Department. He got caught because he screwed up. Experts looking back on the case say it was inevitable, that Jeffrey Dahmer wanted to get caught all along.

After his release from the correctional center on March 2 of 1990, Dahmer signed a new lease at the Oxford Apartments on Sunday, May 13, and moved back into apartment 213 the next day. He was back in business at 924 North Twenty-fifth Street. And he still had his job at Ambrosia, only a straight line of twenty blocks down Highland, all downhill, from his home. On his way to work, Dahmer could look to the right-hand side of the street and see two interesting places—the correctional center that had been his home for the past ten months, and the office of the county coroner, a place that he would one day fill with mysteries and body parts.

Dahmer went in to see his probation officer, Donna Chester, for a long session on June 11 and reported that he had taken home a $275 paycheck the previous week. Although the public records on his probation and parole meetings have been heavily censored, even the bits and pieces that have been left are enlightening. He seemed very down during the June 11 meeting and complained that, because so many things were going on in his life, he was not getting enough sleep. On the family front, Jeffrey said he was staying in touch with his grandmother, but had not contacted his father. By this time, he had not spoken with his mother for years. He spent quite a bit of time talking with Chester about his sexual orientation and said that while he preferred having male partners in sex, he felt guilty about being a homosexual.

Chester noted in the record that Dahmer wasn't involved in any sexual activity at the time and warned him about taking precautions because of the "problems that can arise if he is not careful about his sexual preferences." His answer to the lecture on safe sex was that he planned to remain celibate. Chester suggested he contact a gay rights organization. She made one other interesting note. In the place where she was to designate the supervision level required on Dahmer, she wrote, "Max," meaning maximum.

Three days later, Eddie Smith went missing. The happy-go-lucky Smith, at age twenty-eight, had been living with his sister, Caroline, in a north side duplex apartment. The Smith family was large, eight brothers and four sisters, and everyone knew that Eddie was gay. It was difficult to be around Eddie for any length of time and not realize that he was a homosexual. The makeup he would apply on some days was a heavy clue and, showing a streak of independence, he readily admitted his sexual preferences, as if he didn't care what others thought. But he did, and a jibe from a stranger would hurt him—though his six-foot-three frame and trim 165 pounds might make one assume he could take care of himself. In a photo, one sees a young man with an engaging smile glancing almost shyly toward the camera, a derbylike hat down tight on his head, almost touching his ears.

Eddie told Caroline on the night of June 14 that he was heading out for a night in the clubs. But he wouldn't stay out too late, for the following day Eddie Smith had every intention of marching in Milwaukee's Gay Pride parade, ready to proclaim his homosexuality for the whole damned city to see.

Somewhere along the way, probably in a bar, he ran into Jeffrey Dahmer, who had promised only a few days earlier that he would be remaining celibate and staying out of trouble. Little is known of what happened next, except that a year later, Dahmer was shown a picture of Eddie Smith and said yes, that was one of the victims. The remains of Smith, Victim Number Six, were not found.

When Dahmer confirmed the death, the grim news was not an unexpected development, not for the Smith family. They had expected it. Not only had Eddie not come home from his evening of dancing in the gay bars, and never shown up for that parade, but he was never seen again by a single member of his large family, which had looked high and low for him. Caroline filed a missing persons report on June 23, fearing the worst. Then, what had been a suspicion on the part of the family turned into a terrible sense of certainty when she picked up her ringing telephone the following April.

"Don't bother looking for your brother," said the soft voice at the other end of the phone. She thought it sounded like a white man.

"Why not?"

"Because he's dead."

"How do you know that?"

"Because I killed him."

The short, horrifying call ended there, with a click and then silence ringing in her ear like a tolling bell of certain doom. Jeffrey Dahmer would eventually confirm to police that he had not only made that call, but over the slaughter months, he had called the families of several of his victims with similar anonymous announcements that he had murdered their loved ones.

July came in like a humid blanket, promising Milwaukee another hot summer. As the temperatures warmed, the system was about to goof again and give Jeffrey Dahmer a longer free ride.

In a meeting with his probation overseer on June 25, Dahmer had again appeared depressed, but Chester thought it could be an act he was putting on for her benefit. He had been working long hours, and that, he said, prevented him from having enough time to look for a new apartment. Getting a new place was not a high priority for Dahmer. He liked his neighborhood, where he was an invisible white man amid a throng of people who had black, brown, and yellow skin.

Chester also noted that a probation agent would consider making a house call, paying a "home visit" to Dahmer, but also noted that the subject "lives in a very bad area." Any visit would have to be by two probation agents, not one. It didn't really matter, for no agent ever went knocking at the door to Dahmer's private slaughterhouse. She set Dahmer's next appointment for Monday morning, July 9, at 9:00 A.M. sharp.

He might have told an interesting story at that appointment, had he chosen to be truthful for a change, for Sunday night had been a bummer. One got away.

Dahmer had been cruising the gay bars once again and, outside one of them, chatted up a fifteen-year-old boy. For an offer of two hundred dollars, the kid agreed to pose naked for the tall guy. They got into a taxi, which whisked them up Wisconsin and hung a right on Twenty-fifth, stopping outside the white apartment building. As agreed, once inside the apartment the boy shed his clothes and Dahmer began snapping shots.

But then he put down the camera and picked up a rubber mallet and swatted the kid over the head with it, then tried to strangle him. The frightened boy somehow managed to survive the episode, calming the excited Dahmer, who said he had attacked the boy to keep him from leaving. Then occurred one of the most extraordinary episodes in Dahmer's reign of terror. Looking back over his bloody trail later, this would be a blinding exception to the Nobody Leaves Me rule. For some reason, he changed his mind about the boy. He threatened to kill the youngster if he tried to contact the police, but he let him go free. The boy promised he wouldn't tell a soul. To cap the strange episode, Dahmer, who only moments before had been beating him with a rubber hammer, picked up his telephone and called the kid a cab.

When the boy got home, back on the south side, he broke his promise. He was taken to Sinai Samaritan Medical Center for treatment and, once back home, gave investigating police a description of the man who had assaulted him and an address. And that, apparently, was that. Nothing more came of the incident until a year later, when the boy saw Dahmer's photograph in the media and recognized his tormentor. A year had passed, with police in possession of a description, an address, and a method of operation. While that information apparently sat unattended, Dahmer continued to kill.

The July 9 meeting with Donna Chester provides an astonishing look at how well Jeffrey Dahmer was able to divorce himself from the murderous personality inside of him. Only hours before, he had tried to add a fifteen-year-old boy to his list of six murder victims, yet he was able to show the steady nerves of a safecracker when he was talking to the law. He was sloppy and depressed and talked about suicide after showing up an hour late for his scheduled conference. He explained he had hurt himself falling down a flight of stairs. That's why he was not on time. Chester had not waited for him, but they managed to get together at 1:45 P.M., Jeffrey looking "very rough."

She suggested that he move to another place, out of that "bad area" where he lived, but he said he didn't have the money, that he even had to borrow $300 to pay the month's rent. Chester looked at his latest pay stub, $245, and asked why, if he was making a decent salary, he was having financial problems. Lots of hospital bills, he replied. Bring in all of the outstanding bills next time, she said; we'll work out a plan to pay them off. He went away with a list of places where he could get free meals, leaving the agent with a couple of suspicions. One was that his fall downstairs might have actually been a fight, or a mugging. Two, that he was blowing his money, because at $8.75 per hour for forty hours a week, Jeffrey Dahmer was pulling down about $1,500 a month, plus all of the overtime he claimed to be working. He might have problems, but money shouldn't be one of them.

At no time during the interview did Dahmer say, "Oh, yeah, I tried to kill a kid last night."

Raymond Lamont Smith, also known as Ricky Beeks, was killed six days later. He was thirty-three years of age and wore his alias the way he wore his baseball cap, as a cocky sign of independence. A slender guy with a slight mustache, he had done a stint in jail and had a habit of vanishing for weeks at a time, without so much as a telephone call to his family. He had a daughter in Rockford, Illinois, and told one of his sisters in July of 1990 that he was heading over there to visit. When no one heard from him for a long time, it didn't make any difference. One relative picked up a rumor that he had gotten himself shot. But it was nothing as simple as a bullet that killed Smith, a/k/a Beeks, who became Victim Number Seven.

They met, according to Dahmer's statement to police, at the Club 219, a bar down on Second Street that is squeezed between an aged, empty, white brick office building and a venetian blind company. On the flange of the old warehouse district, the bar takes up the ground floor of a three-story building and is easily found if one is not color-blind. A bright red fireplug stands sentinel on the sidewalk and a purple awning stretches out over the doorway. The upper two floors may be faded yellow brick, but on the ground floor, the name of Club 219 Plus is spelled out in neon scrawl across the purple awning. Inside, MTV blares from television sets. There Jeffrey Dahmer would sit at the long bar, sipping rum and Coke and waiting. Like a hunter waiting for his prey to walk into the killing zone.

It was at the 219 that he had met Richard Guerrero two years earlier, and now he was talking to a cocky young man with two names. That really didn't matter to Dahmer, who was willing to pay Smith, or Beeks, or whatever his name was, to pose for the camera. Green dollar bills. They would watch some videos, have some drinks, and party over at Jeffrey's place. The trip was one-way for Smith-Beeks. This is how police documents describe what happened next.

He (the defendant) gave the man a drink which was drugged and the man fell asleep; that he (the defendant) then strangled the man and removed the man's clothing and had oral sex with him; further, that he dismembered the body but kept the skull and later painted it; further that he (the defendant) identified photographs of Raymond La-

116

mont Smith as being photographs of the man to whom he had done this.

Dental records would later prove that one of the skulls recovered from Dahmer's apartment had once been the head of Ricky Beeks.

Jeff Dahmer was down in the dumps every time he came to see, or telephoned, the probation agents during the month of August 1990. In far-off lands, the Germans were wrestling with the questions of reunification, Mikhail Gorbachev was trying to hold the crumbling Soviet Union together, and Saddam Hussein had thrown a hundred thousand Iraqi troops into neighboring Kuwait, but Dahmer couldn't have cared less. He had enough problems of his own.

He had a stomach ache. Money continued to worry him. He was always depressed and told Chester "the only way he can see out is to 'jump from a tall building.' " She told him suicide was not the answer, then began to explain how the law of bankruptcy works and suggested that he go see a lawyer. But a blackness clung stubbornly to him. As Chester heard him tell it, there was nothing positive and good in his life, and he continually complained about how miserable he was. She thought part of the problem was simply that he did not like being on probation. Well, who would? Most of the notes from the three meetings, at the very end of August and the first of September, were blanked out by the Division of

Corrections before being released, but obviously, Donna Chester had taken some copious notes, once of a phone call with Jeffrey and again in a telephone conversation with someone else involved in the case. Maybe the suicide talk was all show. But he certainly appeared to be depressed enough to believe that suicide might offer a way out. It would bear watching.

September brought with it the Labor Day holiday weekend, a time to party and mark the end of summer, the start of fall. It would begin to get nippy along the lakefront soon, and long sleeves would replace the tank tops and shorts enjoyed by young people in Milwaukee during the heat of summer.

But it was still warm enough at night for people to stay outside late and walk around the neighborhood where Jeffrey Dahmer lived. His apartment building stands midway up the block between West State Street and Kilbourn, beside a couple of similar apartment buildings, also long and narrow, that face out on Twenty-fifth, and across a paved driveway from two old red houses. When Dahmer would walk out of his front door, the view was of the rear of the huge redbrick sprawl of the telephone company, with its huge and thorny metal crown of microwave antennae and other gear that throw and catch radio waves. Still, it is a residential area.

Not so only two short blocks away, for Kilbourn and North Twenty-seventh Street is a busy place, a crossroads in this section of the city, a place where people can meet and hang out until the early-morning hours. Danny's Shop & Save, open every day, sits on one corner, the local shopping stop for area residents, but the life of the place is diagonally across the street, at a yellow-and-red stand called Judy's, where for a buck and a quarter, Vienna pure beef jumbo red hots are sold, Chicago-style, with mustard, pickles, relish, tomato, onion, and peppers, with a grape slush to wash down the hot dog only seventy-five cents. Twenty-seventh Street is a wide thoroughfare, with lots of cars cruising past, more than a few pulling off so the drivers can go inside JR News, an adult book store marked by a flashing neon star a half block down and on the other side of Twenty-seventh from the busy hot dog stand. Action can be had on Twenty-seventh. It is the anchor of what Donna Chester had labeled "a very bad area."

In the wee hours of September 3, Ernest Miller stepped from the home of his aunt and drifted over to the lights, noise, and people along North Twenty-seventh. He was visiting from Chicago to spend the Labor Day weekend with his family in Milwaukee. On Sunday, the second, he had attended services at the Golden Rule Church of God and Christ, where he was known to many. After all, he was a local boy, popular and talented, planning on furthering a career that had already garnered him awards for his ability as a dancer. He was to start studying dance at a college in Chicago in the fall quarter. At twenty-four, Ernest Miller was a smooth and graceful young man who was a long, long way from his roots in Memphis, Tennessee. He was a young black dancer with a sparkling personality and a future.

Then Miller met Jeffrey Dahmer early on the morning of September 3 in front of the bookstore on Twenty-seventh, and that bright future was snuffed out. According to Dahmer's admission to police, he "offered the man money to return to his (the defendant's) apartment at 924 North Twenty-fifth Street in the City and County of Milwaukee, State of Wisconsin; that when they returned to his apartment they had sex and then he (the defendant) drugged Ernest Miller and killed him by cutting his throat; further, that after taking photos of him, he dismembered the body and disposed of the flesh except for the biceps, which he kept in the freezer; he also kept the skull, which he painted after the skin was removed, and he kept the skeleton, which he bleached."

Within a few weeks, Ernest Miller's grandmother began receiving some anonymous, disturbing telephone calls. Once the voice made groaning sounds, another time choking noises, and a third time said, "Help me. Help me. Help me."

By then the neighbors were beginning to wonder what the hell Jeffrey Dahmer was doing in that apartment. There were loud bumps heard at all hours, the sound of Jeffrey cursing, and the whine of a buzz saw. There was also a smell beginning to permeate the air in the hallway. Several people knocked on Dahmer's door to ask what the smell was. He would apologize. The refrigerator was on the fritz, or some meat had gone bad, or he was cooking something that didn't turn out right, or he didn't know but he had noticed a smell too.

Ernest Miller became Victim Number Eight. Dahmer wasn't even halfway through with his carnage.

At the opposite end of the spectrum from the rowdy-howdy atmosphere on Twenty-seventh is The Grand Avenue, Milwaukee's premier shopping mall. All indoors and stretching over several city blocks smack in the heart of downtown around Second and Wisconsin, The Grand Avenue has a bit of everything for everyone, from a tiny smoke shop that sells cigars, to upscale clothiers like the Boston Store and Marshall Field.

The brown bear, with a monocle screwed into his left eye, wears a turquoise derby hat, a dandy orange-and-yellow swallowtail coat, and a big red bow tie as he slowly rides his unicycle, two floors above the bubbling fountains, along a tightrope stretching across the open area of the Speisegarten. On each end of the mechanical animal's balancing pole is a round tray supporting a stein of make-believe foaming beer. Back and forth. Back and forth. A motor pulls him along, the little legs pumping up and down as if he were actually riding the contraption. Most big malls have a food court, a place to munch a taco or a falafel while shopping, but few can compete with The Grand Avenue's Speisegarten when it comes to the amount of beer sold and consumed. Miller's neon blazes in Chichi's Mexican kiosk, Pabst is advertised at Jerry's sub shop, Lite is featured at Pizza Rococo, and a real Irish pub sells everything from Michelob to Hacker-Pschoor to customers who elbow up to the smooth wooden bar at Mike Houlihan's.

Literally thousands of people wend their way through The Grand Avenue's labyrinth of a shopping paradise on any given day, up the elevators, into the dozens of stores; they stroll around window-shopping or just snack at a little round table in the Speisegarten, sipping a brew and looking down on the crowd. For people watching and beer drinking, this was truly one-stop shopping for Jeffrey Dahmer. Before it was all over, he would pick up a couple of victims in the area.

The probation reports for September reveal little, although officials have kept substantial segments of them unavailable to the public. They show that he was pulling overtime shifts mixing chocolate, and the result was a $325 paycheck for one week. He suffered a head cold and was on vacation from September 16 to September 30. He was still depressed, but not as much, and was interested enough to ask how Chester felt things were going with his probationary period, that five-year ordeal that was dragging behind him like some kind of tail. It had only started in

March. Chester told him that he was doing "OK, but he has many serious problems both emotionally and physically that need to be addressed and he is not trying to resolve them."

That meeting was on September 24, which probably was only a few days after one particularly eventful evening during the chocolate mixer's holiday. For on the twenty-fourth, police got a call from the girlfriend of David C. Thomas. Chandra Beanland, who was the mother of Thomas's small daughter, said her boyfriend was missing. They were used to his odd hours, his coming and going at strange times, but they knew that sooner or later he always would come back to Chandra and their daughter.

Dahmer would later tell police that he had met Thomas around Second and Wisconsin, near The Grand Avenue, and made his usual pitch. They went to the apartment in the Oxford and began drinking and talking. Thomas, it turns out, wasn't Dahmer's type, so the two did not have sex. But still Jeffrey laced a drink with a sleeping potion and handed it to his new friend, who drank it and passed out. Then Dahmer killed him because he thought Thomas would be mad when he woke up.

That wasn't about to happen. He killed Thomas on the spot, then dismembered the body, snapping photos as he went about the grisly task. But because the man wasn't his type, his body parts were not added to the growing collection of skulls and bones that Jeffrey kept around the flat. No use having someone around that you didn't really like. The remains of Victim Number Nine were never found.

Thomas was the final person to fall into Jeffrey's trap in 1990. After that, Dahmer apparently lapsed into a sort of winter hibernation. He would not strike again for five months, perhaps upset that killing Thomas had been such a bother. Disposing of a body, having to do something special for someone like that, could be disappointing if you didn't truly like the person.

Meanwhile, he kept reporting in to his probation officer, sometimes by telephone, sometimes dropping by the downtown office. Ironically, this killer of nine people was proving to be a sitting duck for muggers. Two guys ripped him off for a hundred dollars and his bus pass in late September, and someone else stole his wallet in December, but got only four bucks. That made four times that petty crooks had knocked over the same mass murderer. He told Chester he wanted to buy a four-hundred-dollar security system for his apartment. She wanted him to get the hell out of that area, but he said he was locked in by a lease until May.

He confided that he "hate[d]" people who made a lot of money because they were so lucky, while everything turned out so badly for him. She noted that he just refused to look at the positive side of his life and seemed to prefer to dwell on the negative.

One of the positives was his grandmother, who was sticking with him all the way. She called the Ambrosia Chocolate Company looking for him, since he no longer had a telephone, and Jeffrey said it made him feel as if someone cared about him.

In a peculiar November 5 face-to-face interview, Dahmer lied like a thief to his probation officer. He said he had adjusted to being alone when not at work and did not want to go places and meet people. He had his computer and his television and his books and things. She replied that being a hermit was not a good idea.

Thanksgiving came, and this time Jeffrey went over to Catherine Dahmer's home in West Allis. Lionel was there along with Shari. Afterward, to his parole officer, Jeffrey would once again repeat his concern about his family's "attitude" toward his troubles and his homosexuality. That thought would play a significant role in a few months.

On December 5, Jeffrey started talking to Donna Chester about his mother, with whom he had not spoken and to whom he had not written in five years. The probation agent asked if he was mad at his mother and he said no, not that he knew. He simply hadn't taken the time or made the effort to contact Joyce, who by now was far away in Fresno, California.

They discussed the possibility of reestablishing contact, mailing a Christmas card out to her "saying Hi."

The family became a major topic of discussion

125

as the Christmas holidays neared. Psychiatrists say that Christmas, one of those periods most closely associated with the image of the intact family, is one of the hardest times of the year for people having mental problems.

Lionel and David were coming to West Allis from Ohio for Christmas, but Jeffrey said he was reluctant to join them because, even though they were supportive, he had grown uncomfortable around them. He stated that his father was "controlling," that he had nothing at all in common with his brother, a college student by this time, and that he continued to be embarrassed about his criminal offense. He meant the molestation, not the cold-blooded killings he had committed nine times.

With the new year, he was about to send his awful scoreboard into double digits.

CHAPTER ELEVEN

The Rushing Torrent

1991

The new year tiptoed in, a little frightened. The eyes of the world were glued to the sandy wastes of the Middle East, where the United States and a coalition of military allies were building up their forces to do battle with the troops of Iraq's Saddam Hussein. They had given him until January 15 to get his people out of Kuwait and the countdown was on. At the opposite end of the thermometer from the blistering desert sun of Saudi Arabia was Milwaukee, Wisconsin, which was gripped in its usual cold winter vise, with the high recorded on the first day of the new year at a frigid sixteen and the overnight low a flat zero. A line of snow squalls was moving in from the lakes.

On most days, Jeff Dahmer stuck his nose out of the apartment just long enough to get to work, maybe put in some overtime, but on January 3, he traveled through the icy conditions to make his regular appointment with Donna Chester. He talked of money problems and how he got through the holidays.

By the middle of the month, things had deteriorated on the international front as the air war started against Iraq, and from the Rashid Hotel in Baghdad, three correspondents of the Cable News Network—John Holliman, Peter Arnett, and Bernard Shaw—were giving television viewers around the world a ringside description of a city under siege. Major things were unfolding almost everywhere in the first month of 1991. The Soviets were cracking down in Lithuania, China was holding trials for the student dissidents who had led the 1989 prodemocracy movement in Tiananmen Square, and in the United States, an economic recession wouldn't go away. But in Milwaukee, Jeffrey Dahmer was reporting that no major changes had taken place in his life. Same stuff, different day.

Nevertheless, he and his probation officer had a long talk on January 22, and Dahmer seemed finally to have made a link with a woman who was not a relative. He seemed to be trusting her with a bit more knowledge, rather than just lay-ing a biweekly package of complaints on her desk. At that meeting, he told her that the only reason he got stuck in the molestation situation was that he had been drinking, and that after his ten months of jail, as she wrote in her notes, he wasn't about to make that mistake again because he "doesn't want to go back to jail."

Significantly, he also got to the bottom of his homosexuality issue, apparently after brooding about it over the holidays and worrying about how his relatives viewed his life-style. To the pro-bation officer he confided that he "has admitted to self he is gay. Told agent that's the way he is so 'fuck it.'" She wasn't quite convinced and said that, in her observation, he was still struggling with his sexuality.

On the eleventh of February, Dahmer was tak-ing two weeks of vacation, but he came in for a meeting at the agent's office. The subject of their conversation that day has been blanked from the records, except for a notation that he planned to take things easy, get some rest, and work on trying to straighten out his finances.

One week later, he came out of his dormant period, shedding his winter of idleness like a butterfly struggling out of chrysalis. There was a bit of an upbeat mood in Milwaukee at the time, although the city was digging out of the dirtiest weather of the season, having been clobbered by ice, snow, and rain moving in off the Great Lakes.

The stock market that day had taken a bounce

of more than 103 points upward on good news from the war zone on the Arabian peninsula, and the movie theaters were showing some good ones. There was the scary *Misery* with James Caan and Kathy Bates, and Kevin Costner in the bittersweet *Dances with Wolves*; and American theatergoers were getting the hell scared out of them by Anthony Hopkins in *Silence of the Lambs*, in which he introduced the creepy psycho character of Dr. Hannibal "the Cannibal" Lecter. Viewers shuddered at the thought of such a killer, who not only murdered people but disfigured and actually *ate* his victims. And in the final scene of the movie, Lecter has escaped, a monster on the loose. Whew. Thank goodness it's only a movie, they said.

It was doubly ironic in Wisconsin. For author Thomas Harris had loosely based the villain of the movie, a madman known as Buffalo Bill, on a real person, Edward Gein, who had slaughtered and dismembered a number of women on farms around Plainfield, Wisconsin, in 1957. The second point of irony was that walking the streets of Milwaukee was a real-life butchering, cannibalistic serial killer by the name of Jeffrey Dahmer.

Curtis Straughter walked out of his grandmother's home on February 18 and hurried over to Wisconsin Avenue, beside the Marquette University campus, to catch a bus at one of the roofed, three-sided glass kiosks that offered some protection from the heavy rain that was pounding down. A stiff wind blew water into the shelter, making people huddle toward the back as the big drops beat a tattoo on the opaque glass roof. A tall white man was also out in the mean weather, and they started to talk, first about the rain and then about a way to pass the time until it stopped.

Jeffrey Dahmer offered Curtis Straughter money to come to his nearby apartment, and Straughter, a homosexual with high cheekbones and a gentle smile, accepted. Only nineteen years old, Straughter had dropped out of high school and only recently had been fired from his job as a nursing aide. Taking Dahmer up on his deal would at least provide a respite from the bad times, as well as the bad weather. He was horribly mistaken.

Once they got into the apartment and dried off, Dahmer offered his companion something to drink. It naturally was thick with the sleeping mixture, and as the two men engaged in oral sex, Straughter began to loose his strength. Dahmer reached for a strap that he kept handy, flipped it around the neck of the young black man and pulled, hard and steady, until Straugther was dead. Then, while the rain sloshed down outside, Dahmer pulled out his tools again and resumed his usual methods of operation. He dismembered the body of Victim Number Ten, took pictures while he was doing it, then kept, but did not paint, the skull.

It was his first murder of 1991 and it came on a Monday when he was scheduled to report to his probation officer. He did not show up for the appointment, nor did he bother to call and cancel. He was busy.

Marcus Aurelius once described time as a "a river of passing events, aye, a rushing torrent." For Dahmer, the sluggishness of the winter months was about to dissolve into a torrent of emotion and mayhem.

Much has been written and said about what happened to Jeffrey Dahmer on March 25. The war in the Middle East was done after a hundred–hour ground campaign and was shoved from the front pages by the savage beating administered to Rodney King, a black motorist in Los Angeles, by a gang of L.A. cops. Crime seemed to be on the minds of many people, with *Time* magazine running a cover story on "Law and Disorder" and the Department of Justice reporting that the number of Americans who were victims of violent crime rose to 2.3 million in the year just past.

Dahmer was not taking care of himself. He had dark circles beneath his eyes and his appearance was getting sloppy, but he consistently denied that he was drinking. It seemed that as the sun began to come out for spring, and the temperatures warmed, Dahmer began falling into an isolated blackness. He said he was sick.

Then he dropped a bombshell on his probation agent. Dahmer told Donna Chester that his mother had called him from California and they had spoken for the first time in five years. Joyce Flint was working as a counselor at an AIDS clinic in Fresno and was in frequent contact with homosexuals who had contracted the deadly disease. That made her sympathetic to the plight of the gay community, which had this viral menace hanging over it. And they talked about Jeffrey being a homosexual, with his mother telling him that she was aware that he was gay, and that, to her, it was no problem, he was her son and she loved him.

His mother loved him! The mother who had walked away in 1978, taking his little brother along but not him, had stepped back into his life at a most incredible time. Jeffrey Dahmer was indeed a homosexual, but now he was also a mass murderer, just as deadly to the men he took home and had sex with as any disease—and he killed faster.

Whether or not the extraordinary timing of his mother's telephone call to Dahmer, who felt estranged from his entire family, was what sparked his rage to go out and kill again will be examined for years to come by the psychiatric world. But there is no question that after March 25 he began his final killing spree, jamming seven deaths into a period of a little more than three months, as if he were on a treadmill, running faster and faster and unable to sate his terrible thirst for blood.

Errol Lindsey, a member of the choir at the Greater Spring Hill Missionary Baptist Church, was Victim Number Eleven. The personable nineteen-year-old was the kind of person everybody seemed to like as soon as they met him, his wide smile breaking through hostile barriers. He had been shopping downtown at The Grand Avenue on Sunday, April 7, and returned to his mother's flat on Twenty-fourth Street. Then he went out again, apparently to have a key made, only to drift by the ever-active scene up at Twenty-seventh and Kilbourn, possibly drawn by the sound of the rap music he liked so much coming from a boom box.

There he met Jeffrey Dahmer, only two blocks from his lair. Again, the words of the police report are an accurate, but horrifying, description of what happened next, according to admissions made by Dahmer. "He offered Errol Lindsey money to return with him . . . to his apartment . . . that after they returned to his apartment, he gave Lindsey a drugged drink and after he fell asleep, he strangled Lindsey and then had oral sex with him; he then dismembered the body and saved the skull."

Then, as his timetable began to pick up, Dahmer would kill twice in the same month, with his next victim a particularly tragic case in a pantheon of tragic deaths.

Tony Anthony Hughes was deaf and mute. He could not hear or speak a word. The ever-ingenious Dahmer bumped into him outside of the 219 Club on May 24 and, through a careful conversation conducted with hand signals, Dahmer writing notes, and Hughes reading lips, the usual trap was sprung. For fifty bucks, Tony Hughes agreed to go up to the Oxford Apartments, watch some videos, and pose for a few photographs.

Hughes, thirty-one, actually had moved to Madison, the state capital, the previous year but had rolled back into Milwaukee that Sunday to visit his family. He told them in sign language that he was going out with friends but would be back soon. Instead, he ended up drinking the awful brew served by Jeffrey Dahmer and falling asleep, unable to even scream for help as Dahmer began to kill him. Police say Dahmer claimed that after he killed Hughes, he dismembered the body. He kept the skull. But he didn't do all of that to Victim Number twelve until sometime later, just leaving the body lying in the bedroom in the meantime.

As if the dozen deaths alone weren't enough to put Jeffrey Dahmer in a category with the worst murderers of recent times, what happened next launched the case onto a new plateau of interest. The incident will be forever linked not only to the history of mass murder, but to an understanding of the investigative procedures used by white police checking into incidents involving homosexuals and members of minority communities.

Victim Number thirteen would be Konerak Sinthasomphone.

Not much information can be gleaned from the well-vacuumed probation reports of that period. When Donna Chester sat down with Dahmer on May 13, a Monday, she scolded him for missing an appointment with a budget-planning company and told him to make a new appointment before the next reporting period. A frustrated Chester wrote that he was "a compulsive buyer and cannot manage money."

An interesting sidelight was recorded, however. A man had been strangled to death elsewhere in the Oxford Apartments and detectives had gone knocking on doors to ask residents if they knew anything about the killing. When they came to his door, Dahmer told them, and repeated to the probation agent, that he knew nothing about it. Chester had felt all along that the apartment complex was "a bad place."

Sunday, May 26, came along and Konerak Sinthasomphone strayed far from his usual track. Instead of going to soccer practice at Mitchell Park, the fourteen-year-old boy took the bus downtown to look around, particularly to check out what was happening at The Grand Avenue. So did Jeffrey Dahmer.

Somewhere in that throng of thousands of people, Dahmer saw someone that he liked: a little guy, a dark-skinned Asian, trim and in good physical condition. He may have remembered another little boy who looked very much like the one he was stalking.

Dalmer made his usual approach, offering Konerak some money if he would pose for some pictures, and the boy agreed. Back at the apartment, Dahmer pulled out the camera and clicked off two quick photos of the kid, who was wearing only his briefs. Then, the solicitous Dahmer went and got a drink for his guest, clicked on the TV, and shoved in a cassette. As the picture flickered, Konerak passed into unconsciousness. While he was out cold, Dahmer admitted, the killer had oral sex with the sleeping child. After that, he would later tell police, he went to the refrigerator in search of beer, but no matter how much he moved the skulls around, there was not a beer in the box to be found. He looked over at the boy. Out stone cold. Dahmer decided to walk up to twenty-seventh and Kilbourn and buy some beer. He had plans for later in the evening and he didn't want to be without his alcohol.

But something went wrong. As the tall white man turned back onto Twenty-fifth with the beer under his arm, he saw that the kid had gotten out! He was wandering down the street, naked, and a couple of girls were trying to help him. Dahmer's heart and footsteps quickened and he grabbed the boy's arm, but two squad cars and a fire engine pulled to a stop before he could take the kid away from the girls. However, he did not lose his cool.

The officers seemed to want to get everything under control, and Dahmer thought of a line that might work. He told them that he and the boy were homosexual lovers who had had an argument after too many drinks. The Oriental fellow, he said, had done this before, drinking too much and then raving.

The three policemen escorted the two of them back to the apartment building, where two tall flagpoles stood empty on a narrow lawn. A chest-high hedge stood along the width of the four-story building, and a single outside light, a glowing ball atop a green stanchion, provided illumination at the glass front door just off the paved driveway. Four other lights, affixed at the second-floor level along the narrow, white-painted front of the building, brightened the scene only slightly.

They all went to apartment number 213, where Dahmer sold them a bill of goods, literally smooth-talking his way out of what should have been an impossible jam. While Konerak sat on the sofa, wrapped in a blanket, Dahmer played the role of his life. Not only was a live victim sitting over there by the aquarium, but the body of Tony Hughes was still in the next room. But he did it. He actually talked his way out of it! The police left his apartment.

When he closed the door, knowing that he had won, he began that metamorphosis that changed him almost immediately from a reasonable guy, able to chat up a couple of cops, to a terrible ogre with a furious fire in his belly. He quickly did the locks on the door and turned toward the shuddering child across the room. Konerak saw those big, glazed eyes and the face of death coming at him and was afraid. But there was nothing he could do. The drug held him down, as the police walked away.

While the cops were downstairs joking with the dispatcher about having to be "deloused" after settling the misunderstanding between a couple of gays, Jeffrey Dahmer strangled Konerak Sinthasomphone almost over their heads. He then proceeded to have oral sex with the corpse and brought out his camera for some more pictures. Later, he would begin an evening of cutting up not one, but two bodies. Both skulls were added to his growing collection. The make-believe Hannibal Lecter had nothing on the real-life Jeffrey Dahmer.

And still it wasn't over. Indeed, the death machine was just about to shift into high gear.

The probation reports for the period are mostly blanked out, indicating the sensitivity of whatever the agent and subject were discussing at the time. He continued to say he wasn't drinking, a blatant lie, and that he was not sexually involved. But things must have been spiraling downward because the probation agent wrote that she was planning to talk to the Salvation Army about possible housing for Dahmer. Things finally were falling off the rails at work, and the knowledge that he stood a chance of being fired preyed heavily on Dahmer's mind. The state, whose agents had never visited the bloodstained living quarters of the serial killer, still checked the "maximum" box on the type of supervision he was to be receiving.

Matt Turner, twenty, stumbled into the path of the out-of-control Dahmer next, down the road in Chicago during the Gay Pride parade. The young black man had been living in a halfway house for runaway teens at the time, and was flattered by the attention being paid to him by the slender white man at his side. Jeffrey Dahmer would tell police that he offered Turner, who was also known as Donald Montrell, the frequently accepted bait of money for posing and promised they would also watch some special videos Dahmer had collected. A Greyhoud bus brought them north from Chicago to Milwaukee, where the pair piled into a City Vet cab that ferried them over to Twenty-fifth Street.

Dahmer offered a drink. Sure, said Turner. A few gulps and he was out like a light and Dahmer picked up his favorite strap and put it around the throat of the gay black man and tightened it slowly until Turner was breathing no more. Later, he would dismember the body, putting the severed head into his freezer. He later identified Turner as one of those he had killed. Victim Number Fourteen.

Friday, July 5, came, part of a long Independence Day holiday weekend. The Bel Aires, a rhythm-and-blues group up from Columbia, Missouri, was playing a free noon concert at the Milwaukee Performing Arts Center, but Jeffrey Dahmer could not have cared less. He was on the road, down to Chicago again, where he ended up at a dance club on Wells Street, having a few drinks at Carol's, where he met Jeremiah Weinberger, a likable twenty-three-year-old man who did not hesitate to spend some time with Dahmer.

The approach by now was standard for Dahmer, who offered money, pictures, and videos.

As the nation went ablaze in weekend patriotic parades to celebrate the victory of Desert Storm, Dahmer and Weinberger rode a Greyhound bus to Milwaukee and hopped a cab over to Twenty-fifth Street. Then something slightly different happened. Dahmer let Weinberger live longer than normal after the door was closed. They spent all of Saturday together, engaging in oral sex. But on Sunday, Weinberger made that worst of mistakes. The clock was ticking toward Monday morning and Chicago was a long way down the road. He said he had to go. Here, said Jeffrey. Have a drink.

He pounced as soon as the man was unconscious, strangling him, and Weinberger became Victim Number Fifteen. Out came the camera as Dahmer set to work cutting him up, taking more photos as he went along. The head was cut off, of course, and put on a shelf in the freezer. It was getting a little crowded in Jeffrey Dahmer's apartment.

The Ambrosia Chocolate Company was not happy with its longtime employee. Dahmer had been consistently showing up either late or not at all. Even on an overnight shift, continued absences hurt production. Get here on time or else, he was told. Dahmer bought an alarm clock.

But he had a problem in the bedroom besides not being able to wake up on time. There were a lot of body parts around and they were cluttering up what was once a neat place. The neighbors were being a pain, too, complaining about the smell. Dahmer thought it over and on July 12 flagged a taxi. When he came back to the apartment, he was hauling a blue, fifty-seven–gallon barrel for which he had paid more than fifty dollars. He rolled it into his bedroom and very carefully opened the top. A smell of rotten eggs drifted out as the hydrochloric acid announced its presence. Into the vat he began stuffing parts of the various dismembered bodies to melt away the skin from the bones.

Oliver Lacy, a handsome black guy with a small mustache across his upper lip, was hanging out down at North Twenty-seventh and Kilbourn when he responded to Jeffrey Dahmer's casual approach on July 15. Dahmer had time on his hands, but it was again a demonstration of how he could manage a calm facade as disaster nipped at his heels. He had been fired from his chocolate-mixing job at Ambrosia, and panic gnawed at him because he knew life would change for the worse in the absence of the weekly paycheck.

Lacy, twenty-three, had only recently moved to Milwaukee from Chicago when he linked up with Dahmer, agreeing to the proposition of posing for money and maybe doing some other stuff, too. Two blocks away, they climbed the stairs of the Oxford Apartments. Inside of 213, they stripped down naked, Dahmer told police, and gave each other a soothing body rub.

Dahmer brought over a couple of drinks, and in a few minutes Lacy was out cold. Jeffrey strangled him, then had sex with the still warm corpse. The body would be dismembered, but the head was put into a box that was slid into the refrigerator and Dahmer cut out the heart of Victim Number Sixteen and stashed it in the refrigerator, too. He told police that he had planned to eat it later.

The next day, Tuesday, he was on the phone to Donna Chester, spilling out his hard-luck story. His grandmother had been sick over in West Allis, he said, and he had gone over to be with her, staying at the hospital most of the day. Then he'd overslept again and was late for work, and that was why they fired him, Dahmer said. Yeah, he had been drinking, he said.

Chester urged him to come downtown immediately, and perhaps something could be salvaged. She could call the union representative at the company and try to get the job back. Jeffrey said no, he wasn't presentable, that he had not shaved nor taken a bath for three days. Come in anyway, she said. He must have agreed but later did not show up, or so her notes seem to indicate. The situation had reached critical mass. A Jeffrey Dahmer with a job had been bad enough. Without one, he had no anchors at all, but he did have a lot of anger. A whole mountain of it. And the mountain fell on Joseph Bradehoft.

The probation agent had finally seen Dahmer on the eighteenth, shocked at his dirty appearance. His clothes were unwashed, he hadn't shaved, and he kept yawning, as if he were tired. And he had been drinking. She told him, that this wasn't the end of the world, that things are never as bad as they may appear to be. Dahmer thought for a moment. He knew what could make him feel better.

Many buses of the Milwaukee County Transit System ply Wisconsin Avenue, but the Numbers 10, 30, and 31 have the most frequent runs past the neighborhood where Jeffrey Dahmer lived. On Friday, July 19, a very angry Dahmer flashed his bus pass, which gave him a break from the one-dollar-per-trip fare normally charged, and perched on one of the brown leatherette seats. He was mad at the chocolate company; he was mad at the bus driver's constant stop-and-go action as the white bus with the green stripe jerkily headed on its route west; he didn't like being surrounded by all these black people, who were the usual passengers on this run, and he didn't like all the warning signs overhead. You were warned not to smoke on the bus, not to play a radio or tape deck, not to drink, not to litter, not to eat. And if you did, another sign said that undercover cops rode the buses to keep an eye on things. Big deal. Jeffrey Dahmer wasn't afraid of cops.

He decided to get off and walk, and felt the bumpy pad of hard rubber that covered the bus floor pulling at his feet. The double door swished open and he kept his eyes down, watching the yellow stripes painted across the three stairs as he carefully descended.

When he looked up, standing there at the bus stop with a six-pack of beer tucked under his arm, standing there like a gift, was twenty-five-year-old Joseph Bradehoft. He was in town from Minnesota, looking for a job that would enable him to support his wife and three kids. They began to talk and Dahmer said he knew how Bradehoft could make some money.

He made the offer. Bradehoft accepted and they were soon inside the apartment of death. Dahmer told police that the two men had sex before he offered Bradehoft one of his special cocktails and the man passed out. Out came the strap once again and Bradehoft was strangled. The head went into the freezer and the other body parts were dumped into the barrel of acid in the bedroom.

Jeffrey Dahmer didn't know it, but Victim Number Seventeen would be his last kill. Milwaukee didn't know it, but the news that a mass murderer existed in its midst was about to explode with the fury of a winter thunderstorm on Lake Michigan.

The killing spree that only one man knew about was done, but the story was far, far from over.

CHAPTER TWELVE

The Exorcist

Monday, July 22, 1991

To Tracy Edwards, the best thing about Milwaukee was that it was not Mississippi. The weather was pleasant, he had pals to hang out with, and the law back in Tupelo didn't know where he was. Things actually were going pretty well for the thirty-one-year-old father of six.

Even the weather was better up here, at least during the summer. Instead of the humid mass of air that coated Mississippi under a broiling sun, the temperature in Milwaukee, beside the big lake, was only knocking in the mid-seventies as July edged into its final days. At night, it dipped to the middle fifties for pleasant sleeping.

In the local political scene—something of which Edwards was hardly cognizant—Milwaukee Mayor John O. Norquist was cruising toward next April's election. He had no announced opponents, the city was quiet, and he had $403,000 in a campaign war chest in case he needed some good publicity before the voters went to the polls in 1992.

There was the odd incident in Fox Point, where Public Safety Director Gerd Hodermann was being convicted of a fourth-degree sexual assault charge for patting a cop on the fanny while the man was shredding papers.

Closer to the surface of the news that day was that the Milwaukee Brewers had been whipped 5—4 by the Chicago White Sox, and the new state excise tax that had doubled the tax on a case of beer to $1.30 had resulted in fewer shipments by the Milwaukee beer companies.

But what was holding the attention of most people watching developments in the news were the steamy reports coming out of Racine, where an elevator repairman named Joachim Dressler was on trial in a particularly gory case. His wife was testifying that day that she knew her husband was fascinated by pictures of homosexuals and mutilation, but that he was also a very caring person. Dressler, whose collection of pornography was spiced further with pictures and articles about autopsies and videotapes that captured violent death, stood accused of killing and dismembering James Madden of Whitefish Bay, who had last been seen soliciting funds for environmental causes in the Dressler neighborhood a year before.

But Tracy Edwards wasn't all that interested in following current events, other than sports. His basketball loyalty was proclaimed by the blue insignia on his baseball cap and tank top—the snarling blue bulldog of the Georgetown Hoyas. Little was he aware, on that pleasant Monday night when he went out with some friends, that he was about to become famous.

It all started innocently, when they encountered that tall white guy as they hung out at the busy Grand Avenue shopping complex downtown. Edwards had bumped into the blond dude around the Kilbourn and Twenty-seventh neighborhood several times and they knew each other by sight, if not by name.

Tracy Edwards, surrounded by his friends, did not feel threatened in the least by Jeffrey Dahmer, and the group readily agreed when Dahmer suggested they go back to his apartment and soak up some beers. "The two of us will buy the drinks and the others can come later," Dahmer told Edwards, according to a lengthy interview Edwards gave to the German newspaper *Bild Zeitung*. Edwards paid for the beer.

Before the group separated, Dahmer smoothly lied to the other men, giving them a false address. He had plans for this evening and didn't want any unexpected visitors. Then he and Edwards got into a taxi and made the quick trip up Wisconsin Avenue, turning right on North Twenty-fifth and stopping outside the white Oxford Apartments. Until that point, Edwards still had heard no alarm bells, thinking his friends would be right along.

Once inside the door of apartment 213, things began to change a bit. There was, first of all, an awful smell about the place. And then there were the pictures all over the walls of the torsos of men. Those were odd, but Tracy Edwards had seen worse in his life. He later told the Hamburg-based *Bild* that the pictures in the front room depicted "nothing perverse." Still, he was becoming uncomfortable as he settled onto the sofa while his new friend opened a can of Budweiser for each of them.

There was an aquarium beside the sofa containing silky-tailed Siamese fighting fish that would occasionally tangle with each other in a whirling underwater fight. Dahmer said he liked to watch them as they battled, with one fish invariably ending up dead or maimed. Edwards sipped his beer and figured that watching fish fight was a little strange. He waited impatiently for his friends to come knocking at the door. They never came.

The beer was soon finished and his host got up from the sofa, returning with a rum and cola drink. They watched the fish and talked, Dahmer repeating the same question every few minutes, asking Edwards how he was feeling, if he was getting high. Then, Dahmer apparently got tired of waiting for the drug to kick in; he began to grow upset as Edwards made remarks about getting ready to leave the apartment. Nobody left Jeffrey Dahmer without permission.

As Edwards fixed his eyes once again on the hypnotic submerged dance of the fish, Dahmer reached into a hiding place and grabbed a couple of things he would need for the job at hand. Before a startled Edwards could react, he felt the steel of a handcuff bracelet clamp tightly around his wrist, but his struggling prevented Dahmer from securing the other cuff. Edwards forgot about the fish, as his eyes and all of his senses focused on the shining tip of a big butcher knife that Dahmer pressed against his victim's chest, pricking him right over the heart. The once-amiable face of the white man contorted into a mask of hatred and rage.

"His face was completely changed. I wouldn't have recognized him. It was as if the devil himself stood in front of me," Edwards said. Dahmer then issued a chilling and precise instruction. "You die if you don't do what I say."

The first thing he wanted was to see the body of the trim black man, a body that had been kept lean through manual labor. Edwards began to play for time, trying to remain unthreatening. To please Dahmer, he unbuttoned the top button of his shirt. Dahmer was placated for the moment and Edwards commenced to do a series of bluffs

151

and calls that would last for four hours, as he danced very carefully on the edge of a madman's razor-sharp knife.

Dahmer decided to move the party into the bedroom, the private place where other slaughters had occurred. The first thing that Edwards encountered was an overwhelming stench that seemed to come from a big blue barrel off to one side, an awful smell that permeated every corner of the room.

Then he saw more pictures on the walls, but these were different from the ones tacked up in the living room. These photographs showed the bodies of men that had been carved up. Pieces were missing and the blood and chopped meat were clearly seen in photo after photo. Among the most startling were pictures that showed bodies that had been eaten by acid. Now Edwards had a very good idea of what was in that stinking blue plastic barrel.

There was a movie playing on the bedroom television set. It was about a little girl possessed by the devil. Edwards felt as if he had been marched into a chamber of horrors and was absolutely terrified when Dahmer, the big knife still clutched in his right hand, explained that *The Exorcist* was his favorite film and that they would watch if for a while.

Time passed, the longest minutes of Tracy Edwards's life. He kept thinking of ways to stall, but knew he was running out of options. Dahmer would not delay acting forever. Edwards knew

The face of a monster: accused serial killer Jeffrey Dahmer, charged with four counts of first-degree intentional homicide. (*Milwaukee Journal*/Sipa Press, Inc.)

The door to Apartment 213 in the Oxford Apartment complex in Milwaukee, a chamber of horrors where Jeffrey Dahmer lived and lured his victims to their deaths. (Gary Porter/*Milwaukee Journal*/ Sipa Press, Inc.)

Workers remove from Dahmer's apartment a freezer in which police discovered a gruesome collection of human body parts. (Jack Orton/ *Milwaukee Journal*/ Sipa Press, Inc.)

Also discovered in Dahmer's apartment were photographs of his victims—alive, and dead—as well as cardboard boxes filled with bones. (Jack Orton/ *Milwaukee Journal*/ Sipa Press, Inc.)

Police search Jeffrey Dahmer's boyhood home in Bath Township, Ohio, for what they suspect is the first in a long chain of victims that spans at least ten years.
(Dale Gulden/*Milwaukee Journal*/Sipa Press, Inc.)

In 1975, while walking through the woods behind Dahmer's Ohio home, neighbor Jim Klippel found a mutilated dog carcass nailed to a tree, the dog's head mounted to a stake nearby.
(*People Weekly* ©1991 C.S.)

Joyce Flint, Jeffrey Dahmer's mother. Now believed to be a resident of Fresno, California, Flint and Dahmer's father divorced when Jeffrey was 18 years old. (*Milwaukee Journal*/Sipa Press, Inc.)

Tracy Edwards, whose escape from Dahmer's apartment led police to uncover a horrifying scene of carnage and cannibalism. (Alan Michaels)

Fourteen-year-old Konarek Sinthasomphone was not as lucky as Edwards; his escape from Dahmer's apartment, naked and bleeding, was dismissed by police as a gay lovers' quarrel. Sinthasomphone's remains were found in Dahmer's apartment. (*Milwaukee Journal/Sipa Press, Inc.*)

Jeffrey Dahmer has claimed to have killed and dismembered eleven victims. Among them were:

Former high school track star Oliver Lacy, 23, whose heart Dahmer had saved to eat and whose body was found in Dahmer's freezer. (Ned Vespa/*Milwaukee Journal*/ Sipa Press, Inc.)

Nineteen-year-old Errol Lindsey. (*Milwaukee Journal*/Sipa Press, Inc.)

Thirty-one-year-old Anthony Hughes. (*Milwaukee Journal*/ Sipa Press, Inc.)

Police photograph of Jeffrey Dahmer from a 1981 arrest on charges of public drunkenness. He was arrested again in 1988 and convicted of second-degree sexual assault involving a thirteen-year-old boy. (Jack Orton/*Milwaukee Journal*/Sipa Press, Inc.)

Dahmer in court with his attorney, Gerald Boyle. (Jack Orton/*Milwaukee Journal*/Sipa Press, Inc.)

Jeffrey Dahmer, having confessed to murder, dismemberment, and cannibalism, awaits his day in court.
(Jack Orton/*Milwaukee Journal*/Sipa Press, Inc.)

that if he didn't do something, he would soon be a dead man, with his picture joining the bloody gallery already on this strange white man's walls.

Tracy was careful as he made several trips to the bathroom, trying not to excite Dahmer into a rage but at the same time scanning the rooms, checking for possible escape routes. He had to get away, undo the door locks and get out of this charnel house, and that would take time because Dahmer obviously was not going to let him walk out of there free.

The turning point came in an instant, when Dahmer forced Edwards to the floor beside the bed and told him he was going to cut out his heart and eat it. Edwards knew that the time was now. Dahmer was going to start slicing him up like a chicken, but the white man said that before he did that, he still wanted to take some nude pictures of Edwards.

Dahmer turned his head, as if to get some more tools or a camera, and Edwards lashed out his unmanacled hand with a single punch to the face, throwing as much strength into it as his wiry body could muster. Dahmer was jolted by the surprise blow and fell to the side. Edwards squirmed out of his grasp and kicked Dahmer in the stomach, doubling him up.

Then it became a track meet, as Edwards scrambled out of the bedroom and through the living room, clawing at the locks on the door, expecting a knife in his back at any moment.

Then it opened and he was out, first into the hallway, then down the stairs and into the streets.

It was 11:25 P.M., a time when police cars step up their patrols in high-crime areas. Rolling through the darkened area around North Twenty-fifth Street and Kilbourn was a white patrol car with a blue stripe down its side and POLICE written in big letters on the door, above the official seal of the city of Milwaukee. Robert Rauth and Rolf Mueller were pulling their usual four-to-midnight shift in District Three and it was only thirty-five minutes from quitting time.

The two patrolmen in the vehicle suddenly saw a black man running, weaving toward them, with a look of terror on his face and handcuffs dangling from his left wrist. The man spotted them and began waving for help. Tracy Edwards was happy to see the police.

The car coasted to a halt and he ran over to them, a tale of horror on his lips. Rauth and Mueller listened in growing disbelief as the hysterical man unreeled his story. Nobody would make up something that weird. Sounded like a script by Stephen King, not a routine fight in one of the tougher neighborhoods of Milwaukee. Getting out of the cruiser, they walked back toward the Oxford Apartments with Tracy Edwards at their side, talking a mile a minute. A half hour from hanging up their uniforms for the day and all hell was about to break loose about their ears.

The knock on the door of apartment 213 was

answered by the calm and collected Jeffrey, the persona that Dahmer could pull up on a moment's notice and exhibit to the world. He already knew that with Edwards escaping as he had, running away and leaving him alone, someone wearing a badge probably would come around sooner or later. But maybe not! Maybe the black guy would just go on home and forget about him! Anyway, Dahmer knew that he had fooled policemen before, that he had made the entire system of justice jump through more than a few hoops. Maybe he could do it again. Just stay cool, he told himself.

Rauth and Mueller, in their dark blue uniforms of authority, stood between Dahmer and Edwards. They asked a few questions, which Dahmer was able to parry, remaining calm, hardly like the maniacal fiend that had been described by Edwards. But they were alert, ready to go for a weapon or a stick quickly, if needed, for the guy in the door was big, at least six feet. The fact that he appeared to be in control did not lessen their apprehension, nor their watchfulness.

The cops told him to produce the key so they could remove the cuffs from the man who was standing there with them. Dahmer didn't want to do that. For to get the key would mean leaving the safe area around the front door, and once inside the apartment, the suspicions of the officers would be confirmed. They would know something was wrong with Jeffrey Dahmer.

Get it, they ordered.

No. He refused. Jeffrey Dahmer finally lost his

composure and began to physically resist the two policemen, a contest he was certain to lose. In an instant, the three of them were in a wrestling match that spilled them into the living room. It was over quickly, this time with Dahmer, breathing hard, finally in custody, wearing handcuffs himself and being read his rights as a prisoner.

Now that they had the guy, the two cops began to look around at the little one-bedroom apartment. Electrical power tools lay over there near the sofa. Dozens of Polaroid photographs lay about, pictures of bodies that were being chopped up. A bloodstain mottled the bed. A foul stench that could knock down an ox clung to their throats as they looked around. When the refrigerator door was opened, a severed human head, the face still on it, stared back at them. All that and much, much more: the blood and memories of many dead men were calling to them from a nightmare landscape of evil.

They sealed off the room and began the dual process of booking Dahmer and calling into the District Three station. Their report would kick off a scouring investigation of the dungeon that had been presided over by Jeffrey Dahmer and had been uncovered by pure chance. It had taken years, from 1978 to 1991, but the killing spree was finally at an end, not because of any investigation but because a man who was supposed to die had managed to fight his way to freedom and alert police.

Within fifteen minutes, the streets and alley

around the Oxford Apartments began to fill with law enforcement vehicles of every kind. Detectives in sport coats, police officers in their blues, men wearing yellow rubber suits and breathing apparatus on their backs, guys from the coroner's office and the people from the office of the district attorney. The noise awakened the sleeping neighbors, and a crowd began gathering around the blinking lights atop the cruisers and ambulances.

Then, drawn by the police radio reports, the news types began to arrive. Newspaper reporters on the late-night trick and television crews with their big trucks, lights, and cameras showed up, sensing that this one, from what they had already heard, was not just another murder. There was some kind of torture chamber in there. The word had only begun to spread.

Midnight rolled past and Milwaukee entered a new day, Tuesday, July 23, a day that it would not soon forget as the ghastly news emerged. A serial killer had stalked the city, a pitiless murderer who had killed almost at will, and nobody had even known about it. The body count began to rise throughout the morning, as authorities sorted through the bits of human carnage stashed all over Dahmer's tiny flat.

The first firm total came simply from counting the heads. There were seven skulls and four heads that still had flesh on them. Medical Examiner Jeffrey Jentzen made it official. The bodies of at least eleven distinct individuals had been found.

The gore was overwhelming, even to professional law enforcement officers and people from the coroner's office, who are inured to the intrinsic awfulness of death. In the refrigerator they found the head, in a box on the bottom shelf. Beside it was an opened box of baking soda that helped to soak up the odor of decomposition. The upper freezer compartment contained some unidentified meat in plastic bags, including a human heart. In the nearby floor freezer, three more heads were found, enclosed in garbage bags that had been neatly secured with the plastic twists.

In a corner of the bedroom, inside a box that had once housed Dahmer's computer, were two skulls and an album brimming with the awful pictures that Dahmer regularly took while he gutted his victims. Beside it, just under the window, was the large blue barrel and its black lid, jammed with body parts and bones.

A filing cabinet beside the bed had two drawers. Three skulls were in the top one and a jumble of human bones littered the bottom drawer. Opening the bedroom closet and searching among the belongings there, the authorities found a kettle on the overhead shelf. In the kettle were two skulls. Another kettle was hauled out into the light from the bottom of the closet and opened. Inside were a male genital organ and some human hands. Several of the skulls had been painted gray and looked not unlike the plastic replicas of skulls that are sold at carnivals and gift shops and sometimes decorate the rooms of teenagers. Nude photographs of men were tacked to several walls. As dawn broke, police began to question shocked neighbors who had been totally unaware of the monster in their midst. The blue barrel was strapped to a moving dolly and two men in yellow protective suits manhandled it down the stairs and onto a truck. Police looked through garbage bins and shook out sacks to examine their contents. They began to put together the grotesque puzzle of exactly who had lived, and died, in apartment 213.

For Tracy Edwards, his part of the macabre drama was almost complete. He had lived through an ordeal he had not expected to survive, had cheated death by keeping his wits about him, and within a few days found himself in the spotlight.

Reporters and television crews came running. Edwards was big news. He had escaped and led police back to Jeffrey Dahmer's bloody lair.

But if everyone is famous for fifteen minutes, as artist Andy Warhol theorized, then there may also be a Newtonian effect at work providing an equal reaction to all actions. For while Edwards's face was flashed around the globe on TV and in newspapers, sometimes with stories printed in languages he couldn't even read, perhaps the most interested viewers were some men wearing uniforms and badges down in Tupelo, Mississippi.

For almost a year, the Tupelo authorities had been wondering what had become of Tracy Edwards, who had been arrested in September 1990 and was awaiting trial on a charge of sexual battery against a thirteen-year-old girl. Like most of the nation, the officers in Mississippi were following the story of Jeffrey Dahmer and the serial killings in faraway Milwaukee, Wisconsin. But when they saw interviews and pictures of the man who had escaped from Dahmer, the man wearing the handcuff and stopping the police for help, they also saw the face of someone they knew, someone who had jumped bail in Tupelo.

The cops in Mississippi placed a call to their big city brethren in Milwaukee, and on August 6, only fifteen days after Tracy Edwards became a hero, he became a jailbird. Arrested on an outstanding warrant for not showing up for a court appearance, he was briefly locked up in a city jail cell. He was out again quickly, on bail, and represented by a public defender who said the whole thing was a mix-up. A hearing was set to iron it out.

In the next building, resting in his cell in the county jail, wearing the bright orange jumpsuit of a county prisoner, was Jeffrey Dahmer.

CHAPTER THIRTEEN

The Killers

Plainfield, Wisconsin, is a little country town that huddles in the upper left-hand corner of rural Waushara County, about 115 miles straight northwest of Milwaukee. It is a pleasant community, a very quiet place. But when the news broadcasts in the summer of 1991 began talking about the slaughter in Milwaukee, memories awakened in Plainfield, memories of 1957, memories of Edward Gein.

For in that quiet, halcyon year when Dwight Eisenhower was still in the White House, just as deer season was opening, Gein went on the kind of rampage that would in later years strike fear in the nation, even when the term *serial killer* had become part of the everyday lexicon. Back in Ike's day, things like that just didn't happen. America, particularly rural America, wasn't that kind of place. Or when such gruesome business did happen, the instant television services that we know today were not around and the pictures of the blood and the bodies were not instantly hurled around the country.

TV and newspapers, however, had done a splendidly sensationalist job the previous year when nineteen-year-old Charlie Starkweather and his fourteen-year-old girlfriend, Caril Fugate, went on a rampage that killed ten people in eight days, including her baby sister. Their escapade captured the attention of the nation, since it stood out as a most unusual crime spree. Starkweather eventually was executed in the electric chair, but Fugate, who once even wrote personally to the White House, asking Ike himself to help her get out, was released from prison in 1976, without any help or even attention from the president. Starkweather, feeling romantic to the last, had said he wanted to have her sitting on his lap when he was electrocuted.

But Starkweather was simply a little thug, leaving a "bang, you're dead" trail across a couple of western states. People didn't quake in their boots at the thought that Charlie Starkweather might be out there somewhere.

Gein was different. A quiet, ordinary man who lived in an old farmhouse in an old farming community, it would be discovered that he was a prototypical mass murderer, a quiet guy who committed unspeakable acts of barbarism upon defenseless and vulnerable women. The idea that an Edward Gein might come tapping at your door some night is the stuff of nightmares.

Gein admitted that he killed and dismembered two women around Plainfield in the fall of 1957. He also admitted digging up the graves of the beloved dead of Plainfield, the corpses of women, and mutilating them. He used the flesh of his victims and the body parts gathered in his grave robbing as sewing material, fashioning vests, belts, and even a face mask made from a real face. He would wear the gory outfit when he tried to summon the spirit of his dead mother, waltzing around in his bizarre home filled with furniture covered in human skin.

Gein was more than a killer. He was insane and committed the worst kind of atrocities, leaving Plainfield in a state of shock when his house of horror was finally discovered. It was into this kind of serial-killer category that Jeffrey Dahmer fell; a person who would strike without warning, creating a fantasy world of his own, not caring who had to die to fulfill his evil dreams. And, like Gein, he was from Wisconsin.

Also from the Badger State is a sixteen-year-old boy who is awaiting trial on charges of killing a family of five, then dismembering and burning the bodies. Another resident is Joachim Dressler, the Racine man who killed and cut up James

Madden. But Wisconsin is not alone in producing killers. There isn't anything in the water or the air causing this phenomenon.

From Ohio sprang Gary Heidnik, who was sentenced to die for his 1988 Philadelphia atrocities. He kept six women chained up in a cellar of horror, and two died. One of the women who died was chopped up, cooked, and fed to his dogs. From Massillon, near Bath Township where Dahmer grew up and made his first kill, came Oliver James Huberty, who was to gun down twenty-one people in a California fast-food restaurant in 1984. Ohio also does not stand alone.

The United States seems to be on a dreadful path where grotesque and mass murders are concerned. It's apparently a growth industry, and what is considered a shocking crime today can be eclipsed tomorrow. Some of the crimes are not even terribly frightening because they are already past history by the time the headlines hit the street. The rampage is done. Only when the killings are known to the public and the police cannot catch the perpetrator does a vise of fear grip a town, a city, or a region.

Richard Speck slaughtered eight nurses, one by one, in a single bloody night in Chicago in 1966. And thirty-three young boys were killed by John Wayne Gacy, who buried them beneath his home in the Chicago suburbs. In both situations, the public did not know that the killings were happening, and was not alarmed. That was the way it was with Dahmer. He claimed to have killed

164

seventeen of the most vulnerable members of Milwaukee's citizenry—children and homosexuals—and was in custody, behind bars, before anyone knew anything about it. Except for the unfortunate individuals involved, there wasn't enough time for terror.

In contrast are the killers like Wayne Williams, David Berkowitz, and Charles Manson. They held three of the largest cities in the United States—Atlanta, New York, and Los Angeles—in sheer terror while they stalked their victims. People did not care to take a chance with a stranger or stay out alone late at night while those men were on the loose.

Manson, of course, became the Godfather of the Mass Murderers, because of his unrepentant hatred for the human race, his orchestration of the deaths and mutilations of pregnant actress Sharon Tate and six others in 1969, and for committing his butchery in California, where the media always stand ready to once again treat the public to the gaze of his mad eyes. The words "Helter Skelter," the title of a Beatles' song scrawled in blood at the scene of the Manson family's crime, left an indelible imprint on the American psyche.

Killers with rifles are a somewhat different category. Be it a sniper assault, like Charles Whitman mowing down fourteen people from his perch atop the University of Texas tower in 1966, or a James Earl Huberty blasting away in a San Ysidro McDonald's restaurant, killing twenty-one, mostly children, in the summer of 1984, there is little that can be done when a man with a gun starts shooting into a crowd. If you get out of the area, your chances of survival are good.

But when the silent ones come padding about, that is when terror awakens. People like Albert DeSalvo terrorizing women as the Boston Strangler, the Hillside Stranglers, Zebra Killers, Green River Murderers, and Charlie Manson. The fear of the unknown is blackly fascinating, but the accompanying publicity usually goes hand in hand with a massive police manhunt until the killer is discovered and killed or brought to justice.

Jeffrey Dahmer brought a little bit of both worlds to his spree. He was as macabre as they come, if one believes Dahmer's own words, but he moved unseen around Milwaukee and Chicago. Without publicity, he did not have to fear a reaction from a system of justice that is already overburdened with crime. As long as he didn't do anything foolish, like let a victim escape, Dahmer was able to keep killing with impunity.

The drumbeat goes on, for Dahmer is merely another mass murderer, not the ultimate mass murderer, in the United States. We have too many of them, averaging, in some studies, three mass murders of some sort every month.

"We are definitely leading the pack," observed Robert Ressler, the former FBI agent who became a specialist on serial murderers. "It really has become something as American as apple pie from the standpoint of the sheer numbers we deal with year to year."

However, mass murder has a scale, and the number of people that a single person can kill is limited when compared with governmental slaughter such as Germany's killing of six million Jews during World War II and Cambodia's Khmer Rouge wiping out three million of their fellow citizens. Even U.S. Army Lieutenant William Calley's Americal Division outfit tearing through the village of My Lai, slaughtering Vietnamese peasants, puts a lone killer into a dimmer light. Many people killing many other people is one thing, however; one person killing many people can be terrifying.

According to Ressler, mass murders by one person are not even anything new. He cites a countess in the Middle Ages who enjoyed bathing in the blood of village girls, and another ancient murderer who supposedly killed six hundred boys. The evil monarch Vlad the Impaler had gardens of victims who had been run through by long spikes.

But aside from the fact that these barbarous deeds are done, the question remains of who can commit such an atrocity, particularly in an age when civilization is supposedly at its zenith.

Jack Levin and James Alan Fox, in their exhaustive study *Mass Murder: America's Growing Menace*, studied forty-two mass killers and put together a composite profile of such a person. It fits Jeffrey Dahmer like a glove:

He is typically a white male in his late twenties or thirties. In the case of simultaneous mass murder, he kills people he knows with a handgun or rifle; in serial crimes, he murders strangers by beating or strangulation. His specific motivation depends on the circumstances leading up to the crime, but it generally deals directly with either money, expedience, jealousy, or lust. Rarely is the mass murderer a hardened criminal with a long criminal record, although a spotty history of property crime is common. The occurrence of mass murder often follows a spell of frustration when a particular event triggers sudden rage; yet, in other cases, the killer is coolly pursuing some goal he cannot otherwise attain. Finally, though the mass killer often may appear cold and show no remorse, and even deny responsibility for his crime, serious mental illness or psychosis is rarely present. Most unexpectedly, in background, in personality, and even in appearance, the mass murderer is *extraordinarily ordinary*. This may be the key to his extraordinary "talent" for murder: After all, who would ever suspect them?

Ressler, whose own extensive work has become a handbook for investigators, said that Dahmer was different in some respects from the run-of-the-mill mass killer because he displayed the attributes of both organized and disorganized types

of killers, indicating a more complex personality
structure. "All the buzz words apply to him, but
from both sides of the house. That only means
that he has a mixed bag of behavioral traits. He
would lure victims to his apartment, get people
into his clutches, then he will go into bizarre
rituals such as cannibalism and necrophilia that
are not normally found in your organized type of
offender," he said.

Certainly, no one suspected Dahmer of being
anything worse than a drunk. His total of killings, although only standing at seventeen, may
not top the list numerically, but he will always be
remembered for the butchery, the necrophilia,
and the alleged cannibalism that he inflicted. But
fame is fleeting, even for mass murderers.

Jeffrey Dahmer had not even reached his arraignment date before the spotlight started to
shift away. Only a few weeks after Dahmer was
arrested, Donald Leroy Evans of Galveston,
Texas, a hangdog-looking white guy with a
shock of dark hair across his forehead, confessed
to police that he had kidnapped and killed a ten-
year-old girl from Gulfport, Mississippi. While
he was admitting things, he said he had also
killed maybe sixty more people, dating back to
1977. Police are still attempting to prove his
claims.

The same week, in New York, a jury convicted
Julio Gonzalez of murdering eighty-seven people.
He'd had a fight with his girlfriend at the Happy
Land social club in the Bronx in 1990, went out

and bought a dollar's worth of gasoline, and splashed it around the front door, then tossed on a match. The place erupted in flames, killing dozens of dancers trapped on the second floor. The girlfriend survived.

And in Strathfield, Australia, a masked man walked into a shopping mall, chopped a fifteen-year-old girl to death with a machete, and opened fire with an AK–47 assault rifle, killing five and wounding eight before taking his own life with a bullet to the head.

So it goes.

Dr. Peter R. Breggin, a psychiatrist in Bethesda, Maryland, and author of *Toxic Psychiatry: Why Therapy, Empathy and Love Must Replace the Drugs, Electroshock, and Biochemical Theories of the "New Psychiatry"* (St. Martin's Press, November 1991), has written that nearly all perpetrators of violence began as victims. "They lacked, and continued into adulthood to lack," he wrote,

> meaningful, caring human ties. Typically, they responded to these impairments by adopting exaggerated "masculine" attitudes.
>
> We live in a society in which children of both sexes are frequently abused physically, sexually and emotionally. Often they are neglected and abandoned. People who go on to become violent have been especially subjected to overwhelming humiliation in their

abusive childhoods. They have been ridiculed and shamed, and treated as worthless, unlovable, defective or inferior. . . .

When children or adults are inflicted with these deep humiliations, frequently they want to strike back, to get revenge, to prove themselves, and especially to humiliate others as thoroughly as possible. This can lead to subjecting others to debasing sexual assaults.

Because they have been shamed and made worthless in their relationships starting early in their lives, these individuals are fearful and distrustful of people. They tend to become loners and to be described as withdrawn, while their violence smolders underneath.

Ressler believes there are no kids who are just plain bad seeds. "I don't see it as being any sort of an inherent or evil or genetic type of problem. I see it as being induced by faulty parenting," he said.

Cannibalism. The very word conjures up nightmares and deeply held fears in almost everyone. The thought that you may not only die, but that parts of your body may be eaten by a fellow human being, puts such a possibility in a category of its own. Cannibalism has a private pedestal in the dank halls of fear, and this was one of the taboos that Jeffrey Dahmer allegedly violated. He

171

put a heart in his refrigerator because, he told police, he intended to eat it later. Body meat apparently was found wrapped in the freezer. According to one published report citing an official document, he fried a biceps in vegetable oil and ate it.

Reports of men and women being devoured date back to the planet's earliest legends and are mentioned frequently in mythology. In more modern times came the frightful stories of explorers who ended up in boiling pots, as tribes of hungry natives danced around the fires in darkest Africa and on distant Pacific islands.

Travels by seafarers provided tales of crews and passengers of foundered ships who would resort to killing and eating the flesh and drinking the blood of people with whom they shared their lifeboats when rations ran out. The same pattern was repeated as explorers pushed into the world's uncharted spaces and were trapped with no hope of escape unless they resorted to such a barbarism. Among the most well known examples is the history of the Donner party, which resorted to cannibalism when they were trapped by winter storms high in the Sierra Nevadas mountains of California.

Cannibalism actually was almost condoned in recent years in one extraordinary story, the graphic tale of a plane that crashed on a snow-capped peak in the Chilean Andes. Many of the passengers died, and their frozen bodies were to become a food supply for the survivors in that bleak and desolate place. When Piers Paul Read wrote his book *Alive* in 1974, describing the event, even the august *New York Times* hailed it as "a classic human adventure."

What made the difference, moving the taboo subject from horror to literature, was that the Chilean ordeal invited people to put themselves in the place of the surviving passengers of that crashed Fairchild F–227. If fate had put the reader in an identical situation, would he or she have been willing to swallow human meat in order to survive? It made one wonder.

The pattern emerged that whether the situation involves Greek seamen, jungle explorers, frontiersmen caught in a storm, downed aircraft passengers, or, perhaps some day, astronauts stranded on a bleak planet, the argument can be made that impossible conditions justify what would normally be an act of barbarism. One might be sympathetic to the life-or-death decisions of people marooned in a hostile place, knowing that their own lives might depend upon the choice to eat the dead person beside them.

Of course, all that may be good for coffee-shop philosophers, but it doesn't apply in the world of crime, where cannibalism is simply another act of madness. At first, when Dahmer was jailed, the stories flew far about the possibility of cannibalism, with even the medical examiner saying some of the early evidence found in the apartment was consistent with the possibility of cannibalism.

But that awful term soon began to fade from the legal script. Dahmer was going to be tried for murder. Cannibalism was not even mentioned in the criminal complaints.

CHAPTER FOURTEEN

The Million Dollar Man

Thursday, July 25, 1991

On Thursday, July 25, three days after his arrest, Jeffrey L. Dahmer was brought to court, named in a criminal complaint that accused him of four counts of first-degree intentional homicide.

He was unshaven, with a dark, two-day growth of stubble on his face. Dark rings encircled his puffy eyes and he looked exhausted when he was escorted by deputies into a big courtroom of the Milwaukee County Safety Building, an old structure downtown on State Street that was built in the style of a very large, square bomb shelter. Water stains dripping from air conditioners that have come and gone over the years streak the building's facade like trails of rusty tears.

The first thing that was noticed by spectators—a surprise—was that Dahmer did not come into the courtroom clad in the usual orange outfit of a county prisoner. Instead, he wore dark slacks with no belt and a white shirt that had blue vertical stripes and a button-down collar. It was open at the neck. His dirty blond hair was rumpled, swept left to right, as if he had pressed it down with his hands instead of a comb. Dahmer looked much more like a slightly soiled college student up before the law for a traffic beef than a man accused of four heinous crimes.

But there were differences that morning between a minor violation and the complaints that Dahmer faced. Some vast differences. For starters, no traffic offense had ever drawn such media attention, at least not since Senator Ted Kennedy of Massachusetts ran off the bridge on Chappaquiddick Island, an accident resulting in the death of a young woman and another sorrow for a jinxed political family.

In Milwaukee that morning, eight tripods topped with television cameras lined the rear of the courtroom; a uniformed marshal stood amid them at parade rest in the aisle, facing the rear door. A phalanx of still photographers, their shutters buzzing and clicking like a swarm of bees, were on the left flank, wall to wall, their lenses glued to the prisoner. The jury box was occupied on that Thursday by newspaper reporters and television people, with a batch of extra chairs lined up next to it in which sat even more media representatives. The crowd had been formed into a thick horseshoe of humanity around Circuit Judge Frank T. Crivello, who sat, black robed, at the far end of his courtroom, presiding over the strange scene. There was not a vacant seat, and even with all the standing room filled in, spectators still lined the back wall, their view of the proceedings blocked by the television cameras.

In front of and just below the judge, clerks and court personnel worked hurriedly at a desk, making certain the paperwork was flowing to its proper place, because the law runs on a river of paper and ink. A gaggle of uniformed officers and other court wardens clustered in a doorway to the left of the judge's high-backed, black leather chair. Two tables faced Crivello. At the front were District Attorney McCann and three other representatives of the state legal system who were to press the complaint.

Just in back of them, at a second table, sat Dahmer, flanked by his lawyers, Gerald Boyle and Wendy Patrickus. He did not wear manacles, even when escorted into the courtroom, something that, when seen on television, would further anger some members of the black community, who felt that Dahmer might be getting special treatment. The lack of cuffs would continue in other hearings, although the clinking that could be heard in the hallway prior to the prisoner's arrival hinted that Dahmer was wearing the steel bracelets until he had to make his entrance.

The hearing was not actually the initial legal maneuver aimed at finally putting him away. The day before, on July 24, an affidavit had been filed by Homicide Lieutenant David Kane to make sure that Dahmer stayed in jail until the machinery of justice could sort things out. After laying out his evidence, which traced the arrest of the suspect and the recovery of body parts in the apartment, Kane had had no trouble making his affidavit stick, with the court swiftly determining that enough probable cause existed to hold Dahmer for a hearing.

Kane's affidavit gave the first official glimpse of the horrors that were about to unfold, as he recounted how Officers Robert Rauth and Rolf Mueller encountered Dahmer and went into his apartment.

(3) That while inside that apartment, Officers Rauth and Mueller observed Polaroid photographs which included photographs of young males who were dead and in the process of being dismembered.
(4) That Officers Rauth and Mueller also observed a severed human head within the refrigerator.
(5) That an investigation of the homicides at the scene led to the recovery of evidence

which included a total of seven (7) severed human skulls and four (4) additional severed human heads on which the flesh remained.

(6) That the resident of the apartment, Jeffrey L. Dahmer, indicated that he had killed the persons whose heads and skulls he had and had dismembered their bodies.

(7) Dahmer further stated that he had met these individuals either at taverns or shopping areas and induced them to return with him to his home by offering money so that he could take pictures of them.

(8) Dahmer further stated that he would drug these individuals and usually strangle them and then he would dismember the bodies, often boiling the heads to remove the flesh so that he could retain the skulls.

(9) Jeffrey Dahmer further stated that he took Polaroid photographs of a number of these persons while they were alive, after he had killed them, and of their heads and body parts after he had dismembered them.

Kane further noted that Medical Examiner Jeffrey Jentzen had determined that the remains found in the apartment were the parts of at least eleven people.

That extraordinary synopsis of what had happened at 924 North Twenty-fifth Street resulted in Judge Crivello approving the motion that the prisoner be continued in the custody of the court. Then he also granted the D.A.'s request for a bail of one million dollars, to make sure Dahmer didn't go anywhere. Boyle, Dahmer's attorney, did not even try for a lower bail figure and said his client had no wish to contest the state's request for detention. Since Jeffrey Dahmer had been fired from his job as a chocolate mixer, it wasn't likely that he would be able to meet such a high figure and by setting it at a million dollars, the court made sure no one else could spring him.

That process took place on Wednesday and was but a formality that led to the hearing on Thursday, when formal charges could be filed against Dahmer. District Attorney E. Michael McCann had drawn up a five-page document that he brought into court that day.

Dahmer listened impassively in the jammed, but silent, courtroom as the counts were read out. He was accused of murdering Matt Turner, Jeremiah Weinberger, Oliver Lacy, and Joseph Bradehoft between the days of June 30 and July 19, 1991. The judge listened carefully as the district attorney described Dahmer's version of how he lured the victims to his apartment, killed them, and cut up their bodies.

A thin microphone sat on the rectangular table in front of Dahmer, but the prisoner remained silent throughout the procedural hearing.

Identification of the victims who were recorded in that first complaint had been made by Jentzen, the county medical examiner, who had not only relied upon the expertise of his own office, but also had summoned help. Forensic odontologist Dr. L. T. Johnson and Wayne Peterson, a specialist with the City of Milwaukee Police Department, Bureau of Identification, joined in the hurried, horrible task of testing parts of dismembered corpses to determine who they once had been.

Weinberger was identified by comparing dental records with one of the human heads taken from the freezer. The names of Lacy, Bradehoft, and Turner, who was also known as Donald Montrell, turned up from fingerprints lifted from hands that had been found in the apartment. Lacy, the sixteenth to die, was the first to be positively identified.

The state now had four names. Eventually, they would increase that total. Dahmer claimed he had killed seventeen and one of those was in Ohio, beyond the jurisdiction of the local authorities. That left sixteen dead people for the Milwaukee authorities to identify and to build a case around. And at this point, they had only four.

In addition to the killings, the prosecution threw in a charge of something called "habitual criminality," which said Dahmer was a repeat offender, because he was still serving out his probation from an earlier offense while he murdered all of these people. By becoming a serial murderer, he had violated the terms of the five-year probationary sentence that had been mandated for the molestation of the Laotian boy. For that, too, he must pay.

McCann was asking for a mandatory life sentence on each of the four homicides, each a Class A felony in legal terminology. For the habitual-criminality offense, he wanted another ten years tacked on to each sentence. The four murder counts were strong, particularly since Dahmer, when not in court or in his cell, was sitting in an interrogation room, apparently giving police every detail he could remember about the deaths. In a nearby building, the medical examiner's staff was verifying the evidence. Therefore, the last charge seemed almost superfluous, almost a case of the system slamming shut the barn door long after the horse had run away. They had finally stumbled across a killer who had slipped through their fingers so many times, and now they would throw the book at him. Life plus ten, four times. That was McCann's target.

After the court session on Thursday, Dahmer was returned to jail and sat down for more talks with investigators, who were listening with growing incredulity to the story spilling from his lips as he smoked one cigarette after another. If he couldn't have his liquor around, at least a substitute addiction was being allowed. The police were showing him pictures of people who had been reported missing and sometimes he would look more closely at one, and pinpoint a victim. Notes would be made and the strange conversation would continue, but the expressionless eyes still revealed little about the man inside of Jeffrey Dahmer.

However, there was one jarring moment early

on. Investigators reported that Dahmer seemed genuinely surprised when he was told that the Laotian boy he had gone to jail for fondling was an older brother of the fourteen-year-old Laotian boy whose name was among those he was saying he had killed.

Gerald P. Boyle, his lawyer, told a news conference that Dahmer himself had made the decision to come clean. "He said, 'This is my fault. There is a time to be honest, and I want to be honest.'"

Boyle said that Dahmer appeared to be remorseful and that after a forty-five-minute talk with his client, he found the prisoner to be "hurting."

His family was also hurting. In Fresno, California, his mother, Joyce Flint, soon went into seclusion, getting support from co-workers at the Central Valley AIDS team, where she was a caseworker, but being deluged by media calls. Lionel Dahmer, Jeffrey's father, telephoned a Milwaukee television station on Thursday night, criticizing the media storm that was assuming hurricane proportions and was taking a toll on his elderly mother, Catherine, in West Allis.

Lionel said that he had not yet spoken with his son, but expressed a father's anguished love in his brief chat with host Joe Smith on WMVS-TV. "I did not realize just how sick he was. I realize now that he is mentally ill, but I did not know the extent. And I will, as I always have, stand by him in my thoughts and prayers."

Lionel, feeling as though he were caught in a

thick nightmare, would later say that his son Jeffrey was insane.

In New York and in Hollywood, California, another problem arose in connection with the Dahmer case. Paramount Pictures was about to release a new film on August 2, and they were worried that Milwaukee might not be ready for it, under the circumstances. The name of the motion picture was *Body Parts.* Television advertisements were canceled in the area and copywriters quickly altered some of the wording to make it more acceptable.

Meanwhile, police from around the country and in Germany were keeping the telephone lines, the teletypes, and the fax lines humming, sending in special requests. They wanted to know if the man being held in Milwaukee was responsible for unsolved crimes in their areas. Illinois, too, was curious to know exactly where the men that Dahmer said he had picked up in Chicago were killed.

Florida, in particular, wanted to know if he was saying anything about the 1981 murder of six-year-old Adam Walsh of Hollywood, whose head was found in a canal near Vero Beach a few weeks after he was kidnapped. Germany had five dismemberment killings in the area around Baumholder, where Dahmer had been based during his soldier days, murders they were trying to clear up. And Fresno, California, police also asked about an unsolved case. Milwaukee police said that anyone with an open case of particularly brutal proportions seemed to be inquiring whether Dahmer was involved. That included ordinary Milwaukeeans who were worried about loved ones who had gone missing over the past few years.

Inside the city jail, Jeffrey Dahmer was continuing to detail his slaughter, victim by victim, smoking as he talked. The man was admitting to killing seventeen people. He said that in disposing of the bodies, he had relied upon the city garbage collection service because he regularly crushed the bones and dumped them, along with bloody shreds of flesh tied into plastic garbage bags, in outdoor trash containers. The evidence of carnage would be hauled away, courtesy of the Milwaukee taxpayers. Garbage collectors who were interviewed confirmed that there was a bad smell around the bin behind the Oxford Apartments, and that once an ooze of blood-colored liquid had sloshed out of a torn plastic bag, but they thought nothing of it. After a while, a garbage collector gets used to seeing strange things. And the smell? Of course garbage smells.

In a statement issued through Boyle, Dahmer said:

"I have told the police everything I have done relative to these homicides. I have not committed any such crimes anywhere in the world other than this state, except I have admitted an incident in Ohio. I have not committed any homicide in any foreign country or in any other state. I have been totally cooperative and would have admitted other crimes if I did them. I did not. Hopefully this will serve to put rumors to rest."

The short statement was astonishing on a couple of points. In a semantic leap, he had referred to a brutal murder as being merely an "incident," using a word that has nothing to do with death. And in his one-paragraph statement, he did not say that he was sorry about anything at all.

Florida authorities had already established that Dahmer was living in the Dade County area, only a fifteen-minute drive north of Hollywood, at the time little Adam Walsh vanished in 1981. They did not put a lot of faith in the statement of a serial killer and began making plans to question him.

But whatever the shortcomings of the statement may have been, it was important that Dahmer had pointed out the one exception to his murder pattern, the "incident" that took place a long time ago, back where he grew up in Ohio. In the summer of his senior year in high school, he told investigators, he had picked up a hitchhiker and taken him to his home in Bath Township. Then, for the first time, he had killed a human being.

CHAPTER FIFTEEN

Back to Bath

July 1991

The Western Reserve, as the northeastern corner of Ohio refers to itself, baked throughout the summer of 1991 under a blanket of searing heat. A merciless drought crippled agriculture and going outside became a paradoxical adventure, like living in a humid desert. On top of the grim forecast for the crops came the continuing drumbeat of bad economic news on the industrial front.

As the recession had tightened everyone's pocketbooks, people had cut back sharply on purchasing new cars, throwing automobile sales into a spin and dropping more tough times on area industries that supported the Detroit carmakers. That meant restructuring, a fancy name for lay-offs, as business executives sought to stave off disaster. The *Akron Beacon-Journal* published a business survey that proclaimed that about half of the seventy-six companies interviewed had lost money or seen earnings plunge in the previous year.

Over the years, a number of tire companies had been purchased by foreign ownership and only one major plant, Goodyear, remained headquartered in Akron. Firestone was under Japanese ownership, the Germans held General Tire, and many old factory buildings now sat empty and useless, their thousands of windows targets for boys with rocks.

A consumers' group, known as Citizen Action, released a report based on findings of the U.S. Environmental Protection Agency, saying that Ohio rated second in the nation for producing chemicals that can cause birth defects, third in total toxic pollution, and fifth in turning out chemicals that can cause cancer. Summit County itself rated fourth in the state on the list of cancer causers and seventh on the chart of producers of chemicals that can cause birth defects. Unemployment benefits in Summit County soared to $17.2 million from January through May of 1991, some $2.1 million more than the previous year's payout for the same period. And the state's public, four-year colleges and universities learned that state subsidies would be cut for the next year because of declining enrollment. That meant a $1 million hit for the University of Akron.

But Bath Township seemed almost impervious to the slide. The population actually grew from 8,150 in 1980 to 9,015 ten years later, as well-heeled workers from as far away as Cleveland discovered the serenity of this isolated community. Average home prices took a slight dip, but nobody worried about property values, even in the teeth of the recession.

The place had always gone against the tide, even back in the early days when it was owned by the Connecticut Land Company. Originally, in 1806, it had simply been called Town 3, Range 12 on the survey charts, but one of the surveyors took a look at the undulating, grassy land and decided the place should be called Wheatland. Then, in a change lost to history, the tiny settlement became known as Hammondsburgh, which was too much for Jonathan Hale, one of the first landowners. A town meeting argument terminated when Hale thundered, "Call it Jerusalem, Jericho or Bath—anything but Hammondsburgh." So they called it Bath.

From the start, the factories were elsewhere and the homes were in the township. In neighboring Ghent, Yellow Creek provided the power for the early sawmills, distilleries, and flour and cotton mills. People rode over to work there, then rode back to their homes in Bath Township. Decades passed, but the pattern remained.

In 1991, as Bath Township sweated through the sultry dog days of summer, Jeffrey Dahmer, from his Milwaukee interrogation room, suddenly reminded everyone that he, too, once lived in Bath. For the first few days of his arrest for multiple murders, there had been talk, of course, about the local boy, mostly just the gossipy kind of interest. Local interest took a giant leap forward when Dahmer told detectives that his first victim had not been in Milwaukee, but right in the middle of tranquil little Bath Township, Ohio. He did not remember the name of the first man he had murdered.

Milwaukee authorities called their counterparts in Summit County and immediately Bath Police Lieutenant Richard Munsey and John Karabatsos, a Summit County sheriff's detective, began searching back through their files for an unsolved case that matched Dahmer's story. Karabatsos eventually came across a folder that was about an inch thick, one that had hardly been touched for a decade. It was a missing persons report filed on June 18, 1978. The name was Steven Mark Hicks.

With that name and a couple of thirteen-year-old photographs of Hicks, the two officers flew to Wisconsin for what turned out to be an extraordinary interview with the suspect, Dahmer. In three hours of talking over two days, the police were deluged with information about the crime. But actual identification hit a snag when they showed Dahmer a photo of Hicks. After being given a negative response, the Ohio officers slid a second photo forward. Dahmer gazed at it for a moment and settled back into his chair, saying casually, "Oh yeah. That's him."

Karabatsos said Dahmer appeared to be fairly relaxed during the long interrogation, able to keep track of the questions and answers. It was not too unlike a business meeting. "I wasn't grossed out or anything. Jeffrey is a very intelligent person. He had very excellent recall," the sergeant would say.

That was proven out when Dahmer began to detail the crime, describing precisely how he had seen Hicks with his thumb out along the Cleve-Mass Road, how he had picked him up, taken him home, and killed him. Then more detail flowed, as Dahmer outlined the ordeal of trying to dispose of the body by burial and dismemberment and how he couldn't make up his mind at the time how to get rid of the evidence.

Finally, Dahmer told the amazed officers how he had stood beneath the trees and turned in a circle, sowing the crushed bones out into the night more than a dozen years earlier. The police lieutenant and the sheriff's sergeant pressed for more detail and Dahmer obligingly pulled a blank paper toward him and drew a map of his boyhood home in Bath County and of the property surrounding it. He pointed out the room where the murder had taken place, the crawl space where he had chopped up the body, and then drew an outline of where the bones could be found, out by the old property line. To further authenticate his staggering claim, he described in detail the personal items Hicks had had with him. Once he started, Dahmer apparently could not stop divulging new pieces of evidence. He even recalled the name of the victim.

"He gave us information in reference to personal belongings that we didn't even know about," Summit County Sheriff David W. Troutman said. In a news conference, after talking to his man in Milwaukee, Bath Police Chief John Gardner, in an understatement, declared, "Potentially, we have a crime."

Munsey and Karabatsos then flew back to Ohio to lay it out for their bosses and for county Prosecuting Attorney Lynn Slaby. They decided to move quickly.

As Bath police strung yellow tape around the grounds of the home and posted a guard to keep the curious away, Munsey was writing up an affidavit for a search warrant for the home at 4480 West Bath Road and two adjoining properties. It declared that the search of the grounds was necessary to corroborate a confession made by Dahmer, and that officers would be looking for "bones, or bone fragments, blood, trace evidence, including any body fluids, clothing remnants, trash bag remnants, identification evidence and jewelry of Steven Mark Hicks, or any other evidence relating to the murder of Steven Mark Hicks." He submitted it to Judge Glenn B.

Morgan of the Summit County Court of Common Pleas, who immediately authorized the search.

It did not take long to get at least a partial result. William Berger, who had purchased the home in 1978 when Lionel Dahmer moved to nearby Granger Township, told officers that, while doing some yard work several years ago, he had come across a bone. He'd looked at it with only mild interest, figured it was part of some animal that had met its fate in nature's scheme of things, and tossed it back onto the ground. He recalled where it landed and it was quickly hustled off to the office of Summit County Coroner William Cox, who was about to become a very busy man. The ball-shaped bone, about three inches in diameter, was first thought to be part of a human thighbone but actually turned out to be from a dog.

Then a man called police and told them he had done some landscaping work for the Dahmers before they had sold the house on West Bath Road, and that while raking the back area, he had found fragments of bones. He said he had called the unusual discovery to the attention of the family, but that after he'd put them in bags, he did not know what happened to them.

The grunt work began on Tuesday, July 30, as a squad of law enforcement officers and men from the office of Coroner Cox began the hard job of trying to locate the remains that Dahmer claimed were hidden there. They knew they were in trouble at the start, for the area that had been described was so thick with undergrowth that in many places it was impossible to set a boot onto the rocky soil. Ropes of poison ivy curled through the undergrowth and the summer sun quickly made things insufferably hot, even in the shade.

But with shovels, makeshift sieves, gloves, and Ziploc bags, they went to work. The ground was measured off into a grid of squares by crisscrossed red ribbons and yellow ropes. If something was found, the place would be marked by a stake and the bone shard dropped into one of the plastic sacks. Before the first day was complete, some fifty bones were found in the woods, but investigators going through the house, which Berger had vacated, made several significant finds. In the dark crawl space beneath the house, officers sprayed a chemical called Luminol onto the dirt floor. When Luminol contacts a bloodstain, it begins to glow with an eerie, yellow-green hue. Not one, but a number of spots began to shimmer in the dirt, right where Jeffrey Dahmer said he had butchered Steven Hicks. A few bone shards were also discovered there in the dirt. Cox told a roadside news conference after the day's grisly task was done that "The suspect's admission that he dismembered a body in the crawl space is consistent with the amount of blood and bone fragments we found."

They were back at it on Wednesday, with more men and more equipment. While they hacked weeds and sifted dirt, a media circus hit West

Bath Road, with more than fifty news reporters and television people swarming over anyone who even looked as if he might have something to say. Neighbors winced, but kept their cool. Leena Tripp, thirteen, and Stacy Staats, twelve, quickly began hawking sodas and coffee to the news herd at twenty-five cents a cup.

But the terrain remained tough as the surface search continued through six more grid squares. The major finds of the day were four human bones and three teeth, which could be matched to dental records for identification purposes. In an attempt to wrap up the search, more men were called in from adjoining municipalities for the final day of hunting on Thursday, and tactics changed when the platoon-sized unit got to work. Men using metal detectors swept over the soil, looking for metal fillings that might pinpoint a tooth. The howl of chain saws rent the quiet neighborhood's silence as some men used heavy cutting tools to rip away the pesky undergrowth, saplings, and tangles of vines. "We're in lawn enforcement to-day," quipped one policeman, spitting a stream of tobacco juice into the greenery. Others dug six to ten inches into the dirt and dumped the loads into screens tacked to four wooden legs. They found a forensic treasure. Some fifty more bone fragments turned up, giving Cox enough material to begin his work trying to piece together the skeletal remains that were discovered.

He would use a combination of genetic DNA tests, dental records, and the help of experts at the Smithsonian Institution in Washington, D.C.—where they regularly rebuild dinosaurs millions of years old—to try to determine if the findings in the dirt on West Bath Road were indeed human and, if so, whether they once were part of a young man named Steven Mark Hicks.

Watching sadly from a distance was the Hicks family. Their son had vanished thirteen years ago and now the homecoming was turning out to be of the most disastrous sort.

And out of the blue, up spoke Art Swanson, a member of the Summit County Council. He said that the sheriff and the coroner were using the incident to try to boost their budgets for the coming fiscal year. "After they find some bones, they don't have to find them all," said Swanson, who for many years was the treasurer of Summit County and who portrays himself as the watchdog of the public purse. No one seemed to agree with him, particularly since that very month the United States government was making extraordinary attempts to bring home the remains of men missing in action from the Vietnam War.

After the digging stopped and the minicams were gone, normalcy quickly settled back over Bath Township. Hot, expensive cars drove the secluded lanes again, shoppers could go out without being caught in a crowd, and men began wondering about the upcoming football season of the Revere Minutemen. But in the back of their minds, everyone knew that something had changed in the community. Perhaps they were not as isolated as they thought they were.

"It's not as if we are promoting ourselves as being apart from the world," said Trustee J. T. Norman. "A lot of things go on here. The problems of the world are also the problems of Bath Township."

CHAPTER SIXTEEN

A City Divided

July—August 1991

"Is Milwaukee a racist city?" The question was asked several times of people on the streets, not of people in government offices. Their answers were uniform.

"Yeah. Of course it is," replied a white bartender, wiping off a puddle left by a cold bottle of beer in a tavern not far from Jeffrey Dahmer's apartment. "Yes," said the Oriental woman in a flower shop, her dark eyes signaling a remembrance of some past racial slight. The two black teenagers sitting on the fender of a sleek pickup truck in Bradford Park on a Saturday night just laughed. To them, the question was too stupid to answer. Look around, they said. Just look around.

Bradford Park is a charming section of the Milwaukee waterfront, in the cozy North Point section. In the daylight hours, it is a peaceful enough place where families can picnic or watch the water. On Saturday night, it changes. There are two large parking lots there, one close to the water and one just on the other side of the street.

The bigger lot, near the water's edge, is filled with young black people, playing their boom boxes, drinking beer, flirting, and kicking back. The smaller lot, across the street, is filled with young white people, playing similar radios, drinking beer, flirting and kicking back. Black and white, separated by a piece of pavement. During the evening, despite the screeching tires and the clank of thrown beer cans and the laughter, few people will cross that small street to mingle. An uneasy truce reigns.

But following the explosion of reports after the arrest of Jeffrey Dahmer, racial tension was thick in the streets of Milwaukee, needing only a flame to ignite it. Luckily, no one threw a match.

Blacks were openly angry. As was the Asian community. And the gay community. They said that the white establishment, from the office of the mayor on down through the Police Department, had proven, by the way the murder case had been handled, that it did not provide equal protection of the law to people with colored skin or an alternative life-style.

Even the prisoner, Jeffrey Dahmer, they claimed, would have received different treatment had he been a black or a brown man.

They pointed out that most of his victims were black, many of them homosexuals. They said the police did not pursue investigations of such people with the same vigor as if they were hunting the killer of a white college kid.

And angry memories of Ernest Lacy were still strong within the black community, ten years after he died in police custody on July 9, 1981, following his arrest in connection with a rape. Authorities later determined that Lacy was not responsible for that sexual assault.

But the trigger that set off the racial rage was the discovery that Glenda Cleveland, her daughter, and her niece had tried to get police to intervene and rescue a Laotian teenager. The white officers instead allowed the boy to stay with the white man who eventually killed him.

Barbara Reynolds, a columnist for the newspaper *USA Today,* displayed some of the rage felt among the nation's black community as a whole, when she wrote in the August 2 edition:

> In response to a neighbor's complaint, police find a blond, blue-eyed boy, on a quiet suburban street, naked, crying, disoriented and bleeding from the rectum. They listen sympathetically to a black man, who explains

not to worry, it's only a homosexual spat; they hand over the bruised merchandise and leave.

Not on your life would this ever happen. Not in the movies. Not in your wildest nightmares. Police don't behave like that to "nice white people" in good neighborhoods.

And that's the problem. In areas populated by poor people of color, or gay people without status, the bizarre becomes commonplace. They have no rights anyone has to respect.

In the Milwaukee mass murder case, Jeffrey L. Dahmer is a white man. The people who called the police were black. Konerak Sinthasomphone, the terrified 14-year-old, was Laotian.

If police had not taken the white man's word over that of the traumatized brown boy and investigated, they would have found a house of horrors, with human body parts scattered about his apartment. And they would have not only saved Konerak's life but others.

Dahmer's is a classic case of white supremacy at work, a way of life that governs institutions from police departments to courts to the workplace.

The impact of Dahmer's outrage hit very close to home for the black community, partially because he lived among them, a white man in a neighborhood that is 69 percent black. A distrust of police already existed in the high-crime area, one in which even a mass murderer was picked on by muggers. Prostitution and drugs add to the neighborhood's woes, and some blacks are reluctant to call police because of a perception that nothing will be done about the problem. They now cite the Konerak Sinthasomphone incident as inarguable proof that they are not afforded equal protection.

Dahmer's immediate neighbors in the apartment building were stunned into disbelief when they learned what had gone on in apartment 213. Some had knocked on his door to complain about the noises and the smells, but none had a clue that Dahmer was killing people in there.

After the deed, residents felt the pressure of the public spotlight. Not only did the investigators comb through the place, but the media came down in flocks, with one radio station even running its morning show from the apartment across the hall from Dahmer's place. As things settled, the residents began a mass exodus to new quarters.

But marchers turned out in the streets on several afternoons, carrying signs that castigated the Milwaukee Police Department. To vent their anger, about two hundred people attended a rally in the Common Council Chambers at City Hall on Thursday, August 1, and listened for four hours as various speakers condemned the government's attitudes in general and in the Dahmer case in particular.

State Representative Gwen Moore, who is black, said in a news conference outside of the Oxford Apartments that an independent state investigation would be sought of the police procedures the night that Konerak Sinthasomphone died. Alderman Michael McGee hinted that Dahmer might be part of some strange neo-Nazi conspiracy and that the local authorities were covering it up. Others called for the resignation of Mayor Norquist for being insensitive to the community and asked for a federal probe into the way police handled the complaints filed by gays and minorities.

The blacks were not alone in airing their dissatisfaction with the way they contend they are dealt with by police. The homosexual community was just as outraged.

The circle of homosexuals who frequent the bars and clubs actually knew many of Dahmer's victims and felt particularly frustrated. They claimed that police officers ignore information that is passed along by gays about missing homosexuals. Some homosexuals who were interviewed asserted that many gays simply do not trust the police and that cops are generally insensitive toward them.

Hispanics were also angered, as were American Indians and members of every other minority community in Milwaukee. Particularly the Asians, who felt deeply the shocks administered to a single Laotian family by Jeffrey Dahmer. Candlelight vigils and mass meetings echoed with their complaints that Southeast Asians in Milwaukee are not treated equally by police and that the cops look the other way when crimes are committed against Asians.

Almost every segment of the Milwaukee population had a say and a march and a vigil in the days of reaction that followed the Dahmer arrest. And with political blood in the water, Jesse Jackson came to town to appear at a rally at St. Luke's Emmanuel Baptist Church in support of victims' families.

As television cameras whirred, Jackson led a march for those who came to see him on the warm summer evening. The poet laureate of the Democratic Party proclaimed that the situation was not a question of black and white, but a question of wrong and right. He was wrong. To many people, it was exactly a question of black and white, and that was the explosive mixture that the beleaguered Norquist, Chief Arreola, and his demoralized police department, which was being told that nobody out there liked them, were trying to keep from detonating.

CHAPTER SEVENTEEN

The Five Million Dollar Man

Tuesday, August 6, 1991

Outside of Jeffrey Dahmer's cell in the Milwaukee County Jail, a uniformed guard sat twenty-four hours a day, watching the prisoner to make certain he did not try to commit suicide. In that special section of the jail, only one prisoner is put in each cell, unusual in a time when overcrowded jails are the norm around the country. But police had no desire at all to place him among the general prison population, not if they wanted him to live. Since he had killed and butchered so many people, Dahmer's chances outside of solitary confinement would have been slim, particularly since black prisoners might have revenge on their minds when they came near the man who had murdered so many men of their race.

On Tuesday morning, August 6, the guard, with other police officers at hand, opened the door to the one-man cell and Dahmer stepped out, wearing a traditional orange prison jumpsuit over a blue T-shirt, which showed in a dark triangle at the open collar of his overalls. His face was clean-shaven and washed, and he looked rested, with his hair neatly combed. It was time to face the cameras and the court once again. He ambled into the Milwaukee County Circuit Court, slope shouldered and with a blank face, his jaw moving slowly as he masticated a piece of gum and his eyes drilling fearful holes in some of the camera lenses, as if he could see through the film and into the heart of anyone who gazed at him. Three uniformed bailiffs, guns on their hips, marched along with the prisoner this time. There was some cause for concern, for threats had been made. Those who came into the courtroom that day had to first undergo searches by officers who swept hand-held metal detectors over their clothing, and a big dog, a Belgian Malinois named Mirza, had sniffed every inch of the courtroom prior to the hearing, hunting explosives that might have been secreted by someone wanting to kill the killer. The bomb-sniffing nose of Mirza detected only the smell of furniture polish in the courtroom and disinfectant in the adjoining bathrooms. The court was secure.

District Attorney McCann waited at the prosecutor's table with new facts, new names, and new information relating to the massacre, and he had a new request for the court. Judge Jeffrey A. Wagner was on the bench this time, with the courtroom filled with the news media and the usual spectators who turned out for the event. But there was something new. The first rows of the court, right behind the waist-high wooden rail, were reserved for relatives of the victims. The three deputies took seats in front of that rail, separating the audience from the prisoner, who folded his tall frame into a wooden chair, put his elbows on the armrests, and clasped his hands.

There was something odd about him. Dahmer looked comfortable, almost at ease in his new world of confinement. Spectators were seeing a man who had involuntarily gone on the wagon, who hadn't had a drink for fifteen days. Jeffrey Dahmer had been sober for a day more than two weeks. Plenty of rest and no booze! In addition, he no longer was facing the stress of losing his job and having to pay rent. In jail, he got three square meals and a place to sleep and somebody, the guard on the suicide watch, with whom he could talk. The change in surroundings, putting him in jail, had actually resulted in an improvement. A part of his own personal nightmare was at rest. The killing was over. And he had become a very important man. People around the world knew the name of Jeffrey Dahmer, and his picture was everywhere. So it was little wonder that he was looking so different, so much more relaxed than at his earlier hearing.

At his side again was Gerald Boyle, his blue sport coat open and a hand to his mouth, paying rapt attention. The news was not good. His client was being charged with eight more counts of murder. McCann read out the even dozen names of people Jeffrey Dahmer said he had conquered. The drumbeat of accusations was almost monotonous, yet it grew more terrifying with each repetition as the charges were read:

CRIMINAL COMPLAINT

In the State of Wisconsin, Plaintiff, versus Jeffrey L. Dahmer, Defendant, Complaining Witness Donald Domagalski, being duly sworn, says that the above named defendant in the County of Milwaukee, State of Wisconsin

Count 1: First Degree Intentional Homicide

on or about March 26, 1989, at 2357 South 57th Street, City of West Allis, County of Milwaukee, did cause the death of another human being, Anthony Sears, with intent to kill that person contrary to Wisconsin Statutes section 940.01 (1).

Count 2: First Degree Intentional Homicide

during the Spring or early Summer of 1990, at 924 North 25th Street, City and County of Milwaukee, did cause the death of another human being, Raymond Smith a/k/a Ricky Beeks, with intent to kill that person contrary to Wisconsin Statutes section 940.01 (1).

Count 3: First Degree Intentional Homicide

on or about September 3, 1990, at 924 North 25th Street, City and County of Milwaukee, did cause the death of another human being, Ernest Miller, with intent to kill that person contrary to Wisconsin Statutes section 940.01 (1).

Count 4: First Degree Intentional Homicide

on or about September 24, 1990, at 924 North 25th Street, City and County of Milwaukee, did cause the death of another human being, David Thomas, with intent to kill that person contrary to Wisconsin Statutes section 940.01 (1).

Count 5: First Degree Intentional Homicide

on or about February 28, 1991, at 924 North 25th Street, City and County of Mil-

waukee, did cause the death of another
human being, Curtis Straughter, with intent to kill that person contrary to Wisconsin Statutes section 940.01 (1).

Count 6: First Degree Intentional Homicide

on or about April 7, 1991, at 924 North
25th Street, City and County of Milwaukee, did cause the death of another human
being, Errol Lindsey, with intent to kill
that person contrary to Wisconsin Statutes section 940.01 (1).

Count 7: First Degree Intentional Homicide

on or about May 24, 1991, at 924 North
25th Street, City and County of Milwaukee, did cause the death of another human
being, Tony Anthony Hughes, with intent
to kill that person contrary to Wisconsin
Statutes section 940.01 (1).

Count 8: First Degree Intentional Homicide

on or about May 27, 1991, at 924 North
25th Street, City and County of Milwaukee, did cause the death of another human
being, Konerak Sinthasomphone, with intent to kill that person contrary to Wisconsin Statutes section 940.01 (1).

Count 9: First Degree Intentional Homicide

on or about June 30, 1991, at 924 North 25th Street, City and County of Milwaukee, did cause the death of another human being, Matt Turner a/k/a Donald Montrell, with intent to kill that person contrary to Wisconsin Statutes 940.01 (1).

Count 10: First Degree Intentional Homicide

on or about July 7, 1991, at 924 North 25th Street, City and County of Milwaukee, did cause the death of another human being, Jeremiah Weinberger, with intent to kill that person contrary to Wisconsin Statutes section 940.01 (1).

Count 11: First Degree Intentional Homicide

on or about July 15, 1991, at 924 North 25th Street, City and County of Milwaukee, did cause the death of another human being, Oliver Lacy, with intent to kill that person contrary to Wisconsin Statutes section 940.01 (1).

Count 12: First Degree Intentional Homicide

on or about July 19, 1991, at 924 North 25th Street, City and County of Milwaukee, did cause the death of another human being, Joseph Bradehoft, with intent to kill that person contrary to Wisconsin Statutes section 940.01 (1).

Naturally, the charges of twelve heinous murders were accompanied by the redundant accusation that he was a habitual criminal and could get another ten years per victim on top of the dozen mandatory life sentences he now faced. The idea of having to serve an extra hundred and twenty years if he was caught had not deterred him from his murderous rounds.

Dahmer had known what was coming. Wendy Patrickus, the lawyer assisting Boyle, had gone through the document line by line with him prior to the court appearance. When Judge Wagner asked if he understood the charges being brought against him, Dahmer said in his soft voice, "Yes, Your Honor."

In a macabre sidelight, Dahmer was asked if he objected to letting the medical examiner allow the families to claim the identified body parts taken from the apartment. Funeral services could then be conducted. Dahmer could have refused because the body parts were considered evidence and, by drawing that line to a distant conclusion, if he were not convicted, technically the evidence was his property and should be returned to him. He said that he had no objection.

The district attorney had stopped at twelve names because he did not have the identifications and the legal grounds in place to bring formal charges for the remaining five victims that Dahmer had enumerated to police questioners.

He had to tread carefully, because he was building a ladder of homicide cases in which the only living witness was the man on trial. Everyone else involved was dead, and in some cases, there weren't even any bodies to support Dahmer's claim that he had killed them. Even as court was in session, the D.A.'s staff and the office of Medical Examiner Jentzen were still piecing together the identifications, much as if they were putting together a particularly complicated puzzle.

Judge Wagner supported McCann's request for a higher bail, acknowledging the severity of the charges and the kind of violence detailed in the long criminal complaint. He agreed that a million dollars was not enough. He set it at five million instead. Once again, Boyle did not offer an objection. Jeffrey Dahmer wasn't going anywhere.

CHAPTER EIGHTEEN

The Reformer

The Police Department was under a strange siege. Public support for the work done on a daily basis by the women and men in blue, their efforts to keep crime at bay, to keep the city safe, had evaporated like a morning chill under a warm sun. A single tragic decision made on the streets, when three cops believed Jeffrey Dahmer's story about why a Laotian boy was naked and wandering around dazed, had made the difference and turned the department inside out.

The lid was still on. Milwaukee was not burning. But morale within the department had dropped with every new edition of the newspapers and every news broadcast on radio and television. Complaints that they did not dispense justice evenly cut deeply.

But they were in a box. Naturally, the police officers came to the side of their fellow officers who had conducted the investigation on that tragic night. But by doing so, it appeared that they were condoning the decision that led to the murder of an Oriental child by a white man. But they could not, as a group, stand aside and let the three cops who went to apartment 213 be made into scapegoats.

And every day, they had to go out there on the streets again after roll call, and do a dangerous job for a restless population. It was not an easy time for street cops, who reported jeers and taunts from kids on the corners in some neighborhoods.

Police Chief Philip Arreola, on Friday, July 26, had suspended, with pay, the three officers who had handled the controversial call and said whatever action was warranted would be taken. He told a news conference that he didn't know why or how the situation happened, but that a meticulous investigation would determine the facts. Mayor Norquist was quick to step to the side of his police chief, saying that an investigation was warranted and it would be a thorough one.

When the chief was asked why the officers involved had not made a connection between the case they had investigated and the official notice that the Sinthasomphone boy had been reported missing, he had to say he did not know, but he intended to find out.

On the other side, as developments split the city into angry camps, either for or against the police, was Bradley DeBraska, the head of the Milwaukee Police Association. While sidestepping direct comment on the Dahmer-Sinthasomphone situation, DeBraska said Arreola had caved in to political pressure and tossed the three officers to the wolves, in effect prejudging them in the matter before an investigation was concluded. He said it gave the impression that the men had not performed their duties to the letter, a situation that was intolerable in a system of justice in which even a mass murderer is considered innocent until proven guilty. Arreola, said the police union president, should resign.

And that was just Round One.

At the station houses, in the locker rooms and around the coffee machines, the police said the public was getting a distorted view of what had happened on that night, that what was being printed was not the whole story that led to the cops' decision. Not the whole story by a long shot. Outsiders, meaning reporters, were dredging up wrong information that questioned the actions of trained officers. After all, the reporters were not there on the scene that night. And that was correct, as far as it went—but the police sources making the arguments of false information were not on the scene that night either. Their actual point should perhaps have been that the three cops who handled Konerak's situation were not the first people to have let Dahmer slip through their fingers. Why not blame his high school, or his parents, or the army, or the judge who had sentenced him to probation instead of a long sweat of hard jail time?

A particularly painful sting came on Saturday, when the *Milwaukee Sentinel* ran a cartoon by Stuart Carlson on their editorial page depicting two officers in a squad car late at night, writing up a report. The one with a clipboard says, "Can you believe that last call? Some Laotian kid running naked and bleeding in the street, frantic neighbors. Boy, talk about your alternative lifestyle, eh?" The driver turns and replies, "Yeah. Good thing that nice, rational white guy was there to sort things out."

That was it in a nutshell. No matter what was said, the bottom line would remain that Konerak Sinthasomphone was dead and that four other men had later been killed by Jeffrey Dahmer after the cops left the apartment. The officers were by now caught in a vise of their own making. No one actually would deny that something had gone haywire that night. But they could not, and would not, abandon their fellow officers, because it could just as easily have been they handling that terrible late-night squawk on North Twenty-fifth Street two months ago. *There but for the grace of God go I.* Cops don't hang other cops out to dry.

But there was something else at work, something more insidious that began to ooze out when the scab was scratched open. The Police Department had been run for years by Harold A. Breier, a tough, no-nonsense cop who was police chief for twenty years before retiring in 1984 as head of a force of 2,040 officers. Breier had been around a long time and knew everyone, and everyone knew him. The force, however, had been getting steady complaints that it was not being fair to minorities, and in 1975, a court order came down that the Milwaukee police would henceforth hire more women and more minorities. But when Breier stepped down, Milwaukee had a reputation as a law-and-order city.

By 1991, the force had 2,414 authorized positions, but only 1,883 cops, and 80.4 percent of those were white. The reality of politics and budget constraints had squeezed the number of officers assigned to street work even while violent crime increased. Guarding the city of Milwaukee were 1,373 white men and 139 white women; 204 black male cops and 37 black female officers; 93 men and 8 women who were Hispanic, and 25 American Indian men and 2 American Indian women. Despite the catcalls of racism, all of them wore the same color blue uniforms and bright silver badges that made them members of the club.

So it came as a shock when the latest chief took over eighteen months before Dahmer's arrest, arriving from far outside the loop of old-timers within the Milwaukee Police Department. Philip

Arreola was not only a Mexican American, but he was from Detroit! He certainly didn't have to study German in the primary school grades as many Milwaukeeans of his age had been required to do. Having a minority member as chief of police in Milwaukee meant that the members of the club would soon be reading some new rules. When minorities had a complaint, there was someone in the administration building who would listen. Things like racism and homophobia were suddenly on the front burner.

Now a crisis had erupted and he had jumped too quickly, said DeBraska, claiming that the chief had erred in not backing up his street cops. The president of the police union decided that the rank and file would soon cast ballots on whether they had confidence in their chief. And he hinted at a job action to protest the Arreola suspensions. "Job action" could mean anything from an outright work stoppage to a mild case of blue flu, with a handful of officers calling in sick.

The ballots on the no-confidence vote began going out immediately, even as cops in the city's seven districts were angrily learning that the three suspended policemen had learned their fate from broadcast news reports instead of in face-to-face sessions with their supervisors.

Things became even more tense the next day, when it was learned that the three policemen had not only intervened to return Konerak to Dahmer, but had actually gone into the apartment.

The community ceased to mutter and started to scream, and there was little the cops could do but stand there and take it and insist that the chief had not followed proper procedures in administering discipline. Morale sagged even lower.

It seemed that people had stopped being mad at Jeffrey Dahmer, who was, after all, now in jail. He was reduced to the status of curiosity, while the real anger surfaced in the central city areas and was mainly directed against police, who ricocheted it off onto their chief.

Milwaukee was in a spin, with the national media on hand to chronicle the whole miserable thing. The reporters normally would have pulled out after a few days of blood-and-guts stories, but the political dimension that the story was developing was too good to walk away from.

And there was the unwanted link back to the vicious beating of motorist Rodney King, a black man, by a bunch of white cops in Los Angeles. That abuse of police power had been captured on videotape and shocked the nation because of its obvious racism. Now Milwaukee was pushing the City of Angels off the front pages as far as police racism charges were concerned. Los Angeles, at least, was glad that news spotlights only rest in one place for a short period of time.

Mayor Norquist, in a network television appearance on Thursday, August 1, admitted nationwide that Dahmer might have been treated differently had he been black. "From the facts of this case, there's really no other conclusion that you can come to but that," he told NBC News. Meanwhile, Arreola had refined his own stance, saying that the officers had been suspended because they had not followed basic law enforcement practices, and he filed administrative charges against them.

Norquist and Arreola's surprise forum for making new declarations was the graduation ceremony for forty-nine police recruits, who felt suddenly that they were caught in the middle of something they didn't understand. Commencement addresses are supposed to be boring. But the chief and the mayor were standing before them, laying down the law. Norquist laid it out straight. Don't get so cynical that you forget that you are out there to protect the public, and that means everybody. Then they handed out diplomas to the astonished cadets, turning them officially into cops.

Then the state stepped up to bat. The Wisconsin Department of Justice announced it would consider a criminal investigation of the three officers who had been suspended, although State Attorney General James E. Doyle stated that commencing the investigation did not mean that criminal wrongdoing was suspected. District Attorney McCann said the state probe was needed to help restore confidence in the Police Department and for legal reasons. A local investigation might bog the trial down in conflicts of interest if McCann had to call as witnesses three policemen that his department was investigating.

At the end of August, the three officers were cleared of any criminal wrongdoing.

At the same time as the probe was announced, the *Milwaukee Journal* published a poll of how Milwaukee residents felt about their police. Asked whether police discriminated against blacks, some 69 percent of the respondents who were black agreed with that statement, as did 39 percent of the white people interviewed within the city and 39 percent of the respondents who lived in the suburbs. Asked if police were doing a good job, 90 percent of the suburbanites said yes, compared with 70 percent of the white respondents within the city and only 41 percent of the blacks who were interviewed.

Exploring the touchiest part of the situation, the polltakers asked if the three officers who had investigated the May 27 incident involving Konerak had done their jobs correctly. No, stated 93 percent of the blacks interviewed. No, echoed a full 80 percent of everyone interviewed within the four-county area. And 63 percent said Chief Arreola was doing a good job.

Two days later, the *Journal* ran a copyrighted story that disclosed the names and records of the three policemen involved.

Norquist, about the same time, reached into the politicians' bag of gimmicks and came up with a tool that has proven useful in recent years when any political figure, national or local, runs into a problem. He appointed a nine-member blue-ribbon commission to study relations between the community and the police. Marquette University President Albert J. DiUlio was chosen to head the special team. It immediately drew fire from unhappy inner-city residents who claimed that there wasn't enough minority membership, and gay community representatives were left wondering whether any of the nine could represent homosexual concerns. Police didn't like the idea of outsiders looking over their shoulders. Instead of healing the community, all it did was drive the wedge in a bit farther.

Then the union vote came back on the no-confidence balloting and, to absolutely no one's surprise, the Milwaukee Police Association determined that 94 percent of its membership did not have confidence in Arreola. Union officials said that proved Arreola should resign.

In the middle of the uproar, Arreola went to City Hall to argue for more money for his department and to defend his proposed 1992 budget of $129.8 million. Using statistics to underline his points, the chief argued that his troops—the ones who had just said they had no confidence in him—were overworked and tied up with too many conflicting duties. He wanted to put more uniformed cops on the street, particularly in residential neighborhoods. He wanted the city to hire more policemen.

Arreola ignored the vote. He was holding the best cards at the table, and support was growing by the day. Jesse Jackson, in his brief visit to

Milwaukee, applauded the chief's actions, as did other leaders of various minority communities, the editorial pages of the two local newspapers, and the statewide association of police chiefs.

The union vote had backfired. Despite the careful wording that claimed it was a referendum on whether the rank and file had confidence in its leadership, the public saw it differently. Noncops viewed the vote as showing police felt they should not be held accountable when something goes catastrophically wrong. Racial distrust was involved, and the overwhelming vote against the chief was read by minorities as proof of what they had said all along, that the cops had a double standard when it came to dealing with blacks. Supporters of police officers held a demonstration and passed out buttons and thin blue ribbons to raise public consciousness in behalf of the cops, but it was too little, too late. The union had rolled the dice and lost. Arreola, the reformer, was still in office, stronger than ever.

And every day the officers got back into their uniforms, convinced that something was wrong with their world. It wasn't very hard to figure out, in hindsight. Milwaukee had changed. It was no longer the lily-white, European immigrant community that it had been for most of the century. People of every color lived in the city by the big lake, and they wanted a police force that worked for all of them, not just for the power elite. By getting behind the chief in the political struggle that had started with a bad decision on a night in May, a decision that had consigned a little boy to death, the residents of Milwaukee were saying that it was time for the cops to change, too.

CHAPTER NINETEEN

The Law

The dance of the lawyers began.

Milwaukee County District Attorney Michael E. McCann for the prosecution. Attorney Gerald P. Boyle for the defense. As the Dahmer case deserved, it was to be a matchup of heavyweights in the legal arena. But for four thousand votes back in 1968, the chairs could have been reversed.

In that year the district attorney's job was opening up and two young lawyers who worked as deputy prosecutors under District Attorney Hugh O'Connell handed in their resignations to seek the elective office. Mike McCann and Gerry Boyle squared off in the Democratic primary and

McCann came out the narrow victor, eventually taking the general election, too. McCann went on to become a high-profile political figure in Milwaukee. Boyle went into private practice and became one of the best criminal lawyers in Wisconsin, covering his courtroom sharpness with a folksy Irish manner that charmed a jury. His reputation reached out to some odd quarters. When a man said that baseball star Reggie Jackson assaulted him in a bar, Reggie hired Boyle, and charges were never filed.

But the Irish charm is definitely a cover for a tough lawyer. While he was a deputy district attorney, a year before running against McCann, Boyle prosecuted and won a conviction of Michael Lee Herrington for the murders of a young woman and a ten-year-old girl and the near slaying of another young girl. Herrington has been called Milwaukee's first serial killer.

Now he found himself defending Jeffrey Dahmer. Again.

Back in 1989, Boyle was hired by Lionel Dahmer to defend his son Jeffrey on the child molestation charge. He did, and Boyle's presentation was an important factor in Judge William Gardner's decision to hand down a lenient sentence that sent Dahmer to a work-release jail term for ten months and then placed him on five years of probation. That is what defense attorneys are supposed to do.

So when the telephone rang again in the last part of July, it was not really a surprise for him to learn that, with Jeffrey in trouble, deep trouble, the Dahmers wanted Boyle at his side in the courtroom. He did not balk. Dahmer was an accused man, and in Gerald Boyle's book, an accused man has the absolute right, under the Constitution of the United States, to have a fair trial. Everyone deserves to have a lawyer and Boyle agreed to represent Jeffrey once again. At his side was Wendy Patrickus, a Green Bay native who only joined Boyle's law firm in January 1989.

Nothing seemed to go easily in the case, even picking the judge who would try it, a process that should have been simple, but saw some jealousy flash among the jurists.

Judge Crivello, who handled the early procedural hearing, was originally given the assignment of being on the bench for the trial itself. But Judges Laurence C. Gram, Jr., and Rudolph T. Randa thought they had been bypassed in the normal rotation of murder case assignments, and that Crivello was jumped ahead of them in line. Chief Judge Patrick T. Sheedy called a lunch meeting with his quarreling judges and settled the matter, because word of the problem had seeped out of chambers and was becoming hallway gossip outside of the courtroom.

Randa, Sheedy said, had been misinformed. But Gram was correct. It was indeed his turn. Crivello was history as far as the Dahmer case went. And as the case went, so did all of the attendant high-profile publicity. When the third procedural hearing came up on Thursday, August 22, Crivello was not on the bench.

Court Commissioner Audrey Y. Brooks was in charge of room 112, a room on the ground floor of the Safety Building that was smaller than the circuit court chambers upstairs where the earlier hearings had been held. Once again, security was tight and dogs trained to detect explosives snuffled through the room before the doors were opened to the press at 7:30 A.M. More than one hundred people showed up to hear McCann level even more murder charges at Dahmer. Members of the victims' families, some with photographs of their dead loved ones taped to their clothing, sat quietly in the rows behind the bar. Thirty media representatives showed up, quite a few less than in earlier hearings.

McCann, Boyle, and their aides were already in the room, at separate tables, when a side door that had been kept closed was opened by a deputy and Dahmer sauntered in, with an officer at his heels. Once again he was wearing the orange coveralls, but no handcuffs or leg irons.

The prisoner crossed the six feet between the door and his wooden chair in a couple of long strides and once again settled in, leaning back, away from the table at which Boyle and Patrickus were sitting on either side of him. Two other lawyers were with them.

McCann was again heading the prosecution team, which included a police detective captain in addition to two more lawyers.

It was a quick session and Dahmer was in and out in twenty-two minutes. McCann, for the first time, brought charges of murder against Dahmer, for the deaths of young James E. Doxtator, the previously unidentified Native American victim, and Richard Guerrero. An additional charge of intentional homicide was filed for the death of Edward Smith. The two accusations are basically the same type of charge, but Wisconsin law was changed in 1989 and the word *murder* became *intentional homicide*. As usual, there were the habitual-criminal tagalong accusations, meaning that Dahmer now might get another thirty years in prison if found guilty of the three new death accusations.

The criminal complaint stated that in January of 1988, Dahmer met a young man in front of the Club 219 and asked if he would like to make some money "by posing in the nude, viewing videos and having a drink" at the flat where Dahmer was living in his grandmother's home in West Allis. They went by bus, and once there, engaged in sex before Dahmer gave him the sleeping concoction. Dahmer noticed the boy had two scars close to each of his nipples, about the circumference of "a cigarette." Then, in the words of the complaint, Dahmer "killed him by strangling him; he dismembered him and smashed the bones with a sledgehammer and disposed of them; he did not keep any portion of this individual."

The complaint also stated that in the case of Guerrero, Dahmer had met him at the Phoenix

Bar on Second Street and lured him to the West Allis home. "He asked the man to come to look at videos and take photos or engage in sex and the man came with him; they had oral sex at the house and then he drugged the man; while the man was drugged, he killed him and dismembered the body and disposed of it completely without keeping any parts; he recalls that he later saw in the personal section of the newspaper a photo of this victim and a report that he was missing."

Edward Smith, the complaint alleged, also was offered money for sex and to pose for photos when he met Dahmer outside the Phoenix Bar. They took a cab to the Oxford Apartments, where they had oral sex and Dahmer handed over a drink laced with sleeping pills, then strangled him. "He dismembered Smith and took four or five photos of him; he completely disposed of Edward Smith's body by placing it in garbage bags and at a later time he also got rid of the photos of Edward Smith; he further recalls that Smith wore a headband like an Arab." Friends and relatives have confirmed that Smith would wear a "turban-like" head covering. He was called "the Sheik" around the neighborhood.

That brought to fifteen the total number of murder and homicide charges that Dahmer faced. In Ohio, authorities were preparing a sixteenth charge. Missing from the list was any charge connected with the death of Steven Tuomi, the third person that Dahmer told investigators he slew. No remains have been found of that young man from the little town of Ontonagon on the Upper Peninsula, and authorities despaired of ever proving probable cause without Dahmer's confirming identification of a photograph.

Dahmer showed no expression at all as the charges were filed, and offered only a brief response to confirm for the judge that he understood what was happening.

Boyle told the court that Dahmer had formally waived his right to a preliminary hearing, and Commissioner Brooks bound him over for arraignment, still on five million dollars' bail. The defense attorney said later that a prelim, in which the district attorney would have to prove that probable cause existed to try Dahmer on each and every count, would have just been a waste of time.

The legal situation then moved to the issue upon which so much would rest: whether Dahmer was sane—competent and without "mental disease or defect"—at the time of the various killings. A battery of psychiatric examinations would determine his current state of mind, but since both sides would hire their own psychiatrists, even that result would be clouded. Boyle said that Dahmer's state of mind at the time of a killing would be a significant factor.

While broad hints were dropped that an insanity defense was in the works, Boyle continued to play his cards close to his chest. And McCann was not cluttering up the homicide and murder charges with side matters like necrophilia and cannibalism. It promised to come down to whether or not Dahmer was perceived to be crazy when he killed. McCann wanted to be able to prove to a jury that Dahmer was sane and the barbarous acts were those of a cold-blooded killer. Boyle wanted to demonstrate just the opposite.

There was a question about why some deal could not be worked out in advance and save the trouble and expense of a trial. Dahmer had already admitted killing seventeen people, so why could they not just lock him away in a maximum-security mental institution, since there is no death penalty in Wisconsin?

The answer was simply that so much had been made of this case, community tensions had been so heightened by the number of murders and the racial elements involved, that Milwaukee residents wanted to see Jeffrey Dahmer put away in a hard-time prison and not locked up in what one lawyer called "some namby-pamby mental hospital."

With such political pressures in the background, the word in Milwaukee's legal circles was that McCann had no choice but to "go for the gold" and bring to bear the full financial resources of the county of Milwaukee and the talents of his staff of some seventy-five lawyers to challenge the shrewd defense that would be mounted by Boyle.

The case boiled down not just to an insanity plea, but to the powerful issue of whether Dahmer would spend the rest of his life in a state hospital such as Winnebago and Mendota, or in a maximum-security prison such as Columbia or Waupond. Deals can be hard to come by when the spotlight has shined so intensely on a gruesome crime.

Meanwhile, over in Summit County, Ohio, Prosecuting Attorney Lynn Slaby patiently awaited the verdicts from the Milwaukee legal arena. For Slaby, too, had a case against Jeffrey Dahmer—it was in his jurisdiction that Dahmer said he had killed Steven Hicks in 1978.

Slaby has been working on the government's side of the table ever since earning his degree from the Akron University School of Law in 1972, first with the city of Cuyahoga Falls and then with the city of Akron before being elected county prosecutor in 1980. He has been reelected twice and in 1988 was named Ohio's outstanding prosecutor of the year. He does not take such things as brutal murder very lightly.

No matter what the outcome in Milwaukee, Slaby laid his own plans to prosecute Dahmer. The first step was to seek an indictment from a Summit County grand jury on a charge of first-degree murder under the state law that existed in 1978. With such an indictment, Ohio would have a legal hold on Dahmer no matter when the Milwaukee episode was completed. "I feel he committed a heinous crime in Ohio and that he should stand accused, charged and convicted in Ohio," Slaby said.

Slaby took no chances, believing that a life

sentence does not actually mean the person will serve the rest of his or her life in prison. Usually a life termer is eligible for parole in about fifteen years, and no one wants to predict what a parole board, or perhaps a new governor who has the power to commute sentences, might do in any specific case. In addition, if Dahmer were consigned to a mental institution because of a successful insanity plea, a semiannual review of his case might someday seem to warrant his release.

If, under some combination of unforeseen circumstances, Jeffrey Dahmer should someday step out of wherever he may be confined in Wisconsin, Lynn Slaby plans to have a Summit County deputy sheriff standing there to bring Dahmer back to Ohio to serve another long sentence. "We will have jurisdiction when he gets out," said Slaby.

As far as an insanity plea, Slaby contended that in 1978, when Dahmer said he killed Hicks, the planning of the crime and the effort to sequester the remains of the victim would be proof enough that the killer knew what he was doing at the time.

The death penalty looms large in this case. Currently, prosecutors in Wisconsin and Ohio cannot ask the court to order that Jeffrey Dahmer be put to death. Wisconsin has no death penalty. Ohio voters approved one in 1981, but Dahmer said he killed Hicks there in 1978, when a death penalty was not on the Ohio books. Since that was the law prevailing at the time, it is the one that would be used in any Ohio trial.

But Illinois, Florida, and California have shown interest in Dahmer's whereabouts at certain times because of murders in those states or victims being picked up in them. All three have death penalties. Several lawyers have speculated that one of Boyle's tasks is to keep Dahmer from going on trial in any of the thirty-seven states that have a death penalty.

That can be done by letting the Milwaukee case run its course. The worst that can happen is that Dahmer would get a string of life sentences (plus the muddle of extra years on the habitual-criminal charge). And a successful insanity defense might even land Dahmer in a secure psychiatric hospital. A deal could be cut between the state and the defendant at almost any time.

In Madison, the state capital of Wisconsin, legislators began having new thoughts on that absence of a death penalty. Spurred by the dismemberment of the slain victims, Republican Senator Joanne Huelsman from Waukesha said such a crime deserves the most severe penalty and reintroduced the death penalty legislation she had carried unsuccessfully in the last three sessions. Three such bills, all hers, languished in committee during the 1991 legislative session. The Wisconsin legislature banned capital punishment in 1853 after a hanging execution of a wife-killer drew an audience of almost a thousand people, and even the bloody slaughter committed by Edward Gein in Plainfield was not enough to restore it.

Since then, no bill to reinstate the death penalty has made it to the floor of the legislature. In 1991, Governor Tommy Thompson climbed firmly onto the fence, saying he would, perhaps, favor the execution of criminals for certain types of crimes. With no capital punishment bill clearing the legislature, he does not have to sign anything, or even take a firm stand.

And finally, as night follows day, lawsuits began to flower against Dahmer. Under Wisconsin law, if a judgment is won against Dahmer, then any money he may be paid for the publication and film rights to his life story can be distributed to the plaintiffs, such as the family of one of his victims. Two suits reached for the tidy sum of three billion dollars apiece.

CHAPTER TWENTY

"His name is 'Hate' "

Summer 1991

Big news. When the word began to seep out
that a possible mass murderer had been appre-
hended in Milwaukee, the media sat up and paid
attention. Not only was it a serial killer, but there
was butchery involved, possible cannibalism,
heads found in file cabinets and torsos soaking in
a vat of acid. These are the sort of news nuggets
that can explode a routine police collar into national, even international, headlines.

In its first few days, the Dahmer case was
played in papers everywhere and the nation was

soaked with television footage of investigators searching the environs of the Oxford Apartments for clues. Every station, every newspaper seemed to want to have someone on the scene, knocking on doors, taking pictures as the story unfolded in all of its gruesome horror through the descriptions that Dahmer gave to police. As the body count climbed higher, so did the potential interest and the coverage.

The fever spread to Ohio when Dahmer admitted the 1978 death of Hicks in Bath Township, then crested back in Milwaukee when Glenda Cleveland came forward with her tale of how three policemen answered a call of distress about a Laotian boy, only to give him back to the man who would eventually kill him.

It was a story that would not go away. Newspaper reporters love such a continuing tale, because it gives them an opportunity to explore beneath the story and dig up relevant, interesting facts that can expand and explain. Television likes it because of the gore. So-called file footage of Dahmer's apartment will appear on television information segments for years to come, every time a serial murder story erupts somewhere or the Dahmer case takes another turn.

Once again, the story demonstrated that nothing can match the speed of television for getting information distributed, but that TV copyreaders consistently fall short in delivering a continuing, comprehensive story. For all of the obtrusiveness of the cameras, the lights, the bands of producers and field agents, television has not yet come of age enough to be able to shut down the lights and turn off the cameras when enough is enough.

But TV did play an important role, because people, particularly officials, like to appear on the tube. Therefore, the top players in the drama went out of their way to appear on national television and put forth their points of view, while at the same time putting distance between themselves and investigative newspaper reporters. While inconclusive in its coverage, hurrying so fast at times that the people in the field did not even have time to read the documents on which they were trying to report, television still had its usual impact of showing the viewer where things happened, if being unable to explain why they happened.

In Milwaukee, the local newspapers, the *Sentinel* and the *Journal,* jumped on the story from the start and provided detailed coverage, which was, for the most part, rewritten by the wire services and transmitted to other newspapers around the country and the world. And the coverage caught on, with the nation becoming fascinated by the story of the alleged killer who broke almost every taboo in the book. Reporters swarmed in from newspapers and magazines around the country to examine what happened and, for the most part, ended up writing the same things that everyone else was writing.

Even the *New York Times,* long considered the bastion of conservative journalism, leaped at the story, giving it extensive coverage and coming up with exclusive details.

The Ohio papers covered the Bath murder like a rug, generally playing it in a somewhat understated manner but quickly digging into the backgrounds of the family and tracing Dahmer's early life.

In Milwaukee, however, the local newspapers began to feel a somewhat divided loyalty after the case droned on and on. While doing their job of trying to represent all sides of the controversy and report everything possibly relevant, the papers were also prone to start defending their city's reputation against the printed comments of outside journalists. For example, on July 29, the morning *Journal* ran a story headlined CRITIC SAYS NEWS REPORTS TOO GRAPHIC, while the afternoon *Sentinel* the following day ran its own piece of media criticism, declaring, MOST SAY THEY WANT TO KNOW MORE ABOUT CASE.

On August 11, the *Journal* report summing up the events to that point took a decidedly defensive tone about the "media circus" of reporters from outside of the city and the stories they were writing:

> Milwaukee's dirty laundry is plastered across front pages of newspapers nationwide and on network news broadcasts. Journalists from Italy, France, Great Britain and Germany descend on the city, first for the horrors of the murders and then for the fall-

244

out from [Glenda] Cleveland's phone call. Some of the news coverage is as bizarre as this complicated story.

Even the respected *Washington Post* has added to the tabloid fever. In an overwrought feature in its Style section, the *Post* dubbed Milwaukee a city of "sausage plants and abandoned breweries," described its residents as "big-armed blonds" as solid as mythical "mammoth Milwaukee bungalows lined up on Lake Drive."

But overall, the two local newspapers did an excellent job in portraying not only the unfolding horror of the crime, but the surrounding community issues that surfaced with the story of Konerak Sinthasomphone's abandonment. They broke through the Police Department's effort to cover up the incident, reporting that officers told Cleveland not to talk about it to the press.

The stories went a long way toward putting the situation in focus, but also opened Milwaukee to some ridicule from their press colleagues who drew cartoons for a living. One such cartoon appeared in the *Louisiana Weekly,* when artist John Slade pictured a Milwaukee police car wearing a bumper sticker that read, "We brake for white male mass murderers who knock off the poor, black and gay."

Noting the atmosphere of shame, the *Journal* ran an editorial on July 31 comparing the negative publicity from the Dahmer killings with the legacy that Dallas inherited after President Kennedy was assassinated. The previous day, the *Sentinel* editorialized that the officers of the Police Department did not murder anyone, but that critics were indicting the whole officer corps for the actions of three cops who had been suspended.

So the coverage took on a dual role, partly actively probing the crime and the follow-up and partly showing that Milwaukee was taking a bad rap in the national media. The *Journal's* extraordinary efforts to dig up and publish the names and histories of the three suspended officers contrasted with the hometown-boosting story it led with on the front page of its Sunday edition of August 11, reporting FBI data and declaring Wisconsin to be "safer than most states." The peculiar story's second paragraph stated that urban Milwaukee County trailed many other Wisconsin counties in crimes, such as aggravated assault, drunken driving, and serious juvenile crime, but did lead the state in a few categories, such as murder, rape, and robbery.

For the most part, despite the herd instinct and feeding frenzy that surrounded the first few days of coverage, both in Wisconsin and Ohio, the media did their job. The nation wanted to know about Jeffrey Dahmer and the reporters told them, much to the dismay of civic leaders, governmental officials, and cops who just wanted the whole thing to go away.

In any such news event, there are three primary parts—a beginning, a middle, and an end. This story was over relatively swiftly for something of its complexity and magnitude, primarily because Dahmer's trail of death had come to an end before anyone even knew it was out there. The reporting did not begin with the discovery of body parts and corpses along the lakefront, but with the arrest of a man who said he had killed seventeen people.

Therefore, what was reported early on was actually the middle part of the process—the court appearances, the legal jockeying, the identification of bodies, and the political turmoil within the community. The political uproar began to settle within weeks, and the police situation was getting back to normal by September.

The final chapters are yet to be written and the full story will probably not be known for years, until the trials are concluded and scholars and psychiatrists finish analyzing Dahmer's mental state to figure out what made him go haywire.

There already has been some closure, however, and covering some of those events is one of the toughest assignments a reporter can draw. Much worse than seeing a dead body is having to be among the mourning family, intruding during a time of grief. At times such as that, when the TV cameras begin creeping up on a mother weeping at her son's coffin, journalists should wonder where the profession is heading.

Jeffrey Dahmer left seventeen grieving families in his wake, and each had to plan a funeral, to put a final end to their own part in the drama. One by one, memorial services were held and the words of burial were said for the victims who fell under Dahmer's deadly spell.

But in Ohio, the family of Steven Hicks had to wait for weeks, until scientists could come up with a final, positive identification that the remains found in the backyard on West Bath Road were those of their son. And in Michigan, the family of Steven Tuomi began to resign themselves to the possibility that his remains may never be found.

A special poignancy accompanied the laying to rest of one of the victims. For Konerak Sinthasomphone was something more than just another victim. The little Laotian boy, and his fate, had become the symbol of the entire nightmare.

A memorial service was held on Monday, August 5, for Konerak at St. John Cathedral, and three days later, a special visitation was held at the Becker Ritter Funeral Home, and on both occasions, dozens of people who had never known the boy nor his family showed up to express their sympathy.

The tale of sorrow that accompanies any death was compounded with Konerak because a chance for the boy to be rescued had slipped through the fingers of the investigating police officers. Who could not feel saddened by such a thing? At least one person would soon prove to be as heartless as Jeffrey Dahmer, who had staged not one, but two, attacks on the same family.

Finally, over a weekend, came a pair of memorial services, one a Christian service at St. John, with Roman Catholic priests in their richly embroidered religious raiment, and the other a traditional service that was conducted by Buddhist monks wearing their plain saffron robes. It was an appropriate mixture of the old ways and the new ways, the cultural bridge that Konerak Sinthasomphone was trying to cross.

For a week, at the funeral home and at the family residence, the soul of the boy had been prepared for its final journey in traditional Lao ways. A color photograph of a smiling Konerak was propped on a table, flanked by burning white candles and fresh flowers. A tray containing small bowls of food and a glass of orange juice was placed before the picture, to nourish the spirit until the time for final cremation in nearby Brookfield.

At the Buddhist ceremony, more small gifts were offered before the small wooden casket with brass handles, as monks prepared to escort the boy on his final journey. Konerak, who started out on May 26 for soccer practice in a park, was about to be laid to rest. Finally, the nightmare that had plagued the immigrant Laotian family would be over.

Well, not quite. There was one more slap awaiting them, something that would give their ongoing grief a final twist.

A thick cord of cotton was tied to a handle of the casket as family members knelt in prayer beside it. After the chants and prayers that rang with the clipped words of the Asian dialect, the symbolic rope was tied to the waist of one of the monks from Milwaukee's Lao Buddhist Temple, and with his comrades and the family, he led the way into a chapel for final prayers, the length of rope helping guide Konerak to a peaceful resting place.

Among the hundreds of people who paid their respects to the boy during the various services were a number who reached into their wallets and donated money to help the family. It was not much, but it did indicate that members of the community cared, that they wanted to do something to ease the unbelievable burden that had been laid upon the Sinthasomphones. Mail containing money and checks, some of it sent anonymously, had arrived at the family's home. Strangers, good people, trying to help.

By the time the Buddhist services were concluded on Saturday, August 10, some six thousand dollars in memorial donations had accumulated, money that could help pay the funeral costs and other expenses. The donations were folded into the purse of a daughter, who put it in her bedroom. She would take it to the bank Monday morning.

Someone, a thief with no heart whatsoever, pried open her bedroom window over the weekend and stole every penny.

CHAPTER TWENTY-ONE

Fault Lines

Ashok Bedi is a philosophical man, soft of speech and bred with gentle manners. Such traits make him an ideal observer of what is going on around him, and, combined with the ability to listen and analyze, have produced a respected psychiatrist.

Currently, working out of a corner office in the central administration building of the Wisconsin Psychiatric Hospital, Dr. Bedi is a long way, both in miles and training, from the little village in India where his own personal story began forty-three years ago. But he is linked to his home nation by the philosophy of Mahatma Gandhi, and to his village by the knowledge that it was there that the understated Gandhi mapped the historic campaign of persistent nonviolence that won India its independence from Great Britain.

So it was with a bit of irony that Bedi, when he was only twenty-three years of age, moved from the cradle of Gandhi's ashram and went away to England, the hub of the empire that once ruled his homeland, to finish his medical studies at Oxford University. Five years later, his academic training complete, he answered a recruitment inquiry and came to practice his profession in Milwaukee, where he has lived ever since.

For fifteen years he has treated patients from all corners of this city of immigrants, learning how Milwaukee's diverse population has evolved and where the city may be heading. When the Jeffrey Dahmer case erupted, his position as a student of human behavior and as an Asian American who is a student of the city that has become his adopted home allowed him to provide an in-depth, dispassionate look at the overall case.

Over lunch at a delicatessen, Bedi, a partner in Milwaukee Psychiatric Physicians Chartered, was asked if Milwaukee, a city of many cultures, has remained the same friendly city that European immigrants had always talked about.

"I think it is a European city that is changing its colors," replied Bedi. "In the last fifteen years or so, there has been a gradual influx of Mexican Americans and Oriental Americans, such as the

Laotian and Hmong communities, all of which are struggling very hard to integrate. There is sort of a changing of the guard. The watershed event was the retirement of the old police chief, Harold Breier, who sort of ruled with an iron fist for many years. But he is outdated and was replaced by the new chief [Philip Arreola]. This transition was symbolic of the transition of the city, because the new chief is a Mexican American. That transition of power took place while the city was attempting to grapple with its own transition. They are still struggling with it and there is a lot of resistance to accept Chief Arreola as 'one of us.' "

The psychiatrist was then asked if whites were moving out of Milwaukee, fleeing the city for the suburbs, a phenomenon called "white flight" that has already sharply changed the racial and cultural makeup of many urban areas.

Bedi commented, "That is true. The fastest-growing suburbs of Milwaukee are Waukesha and outer regions. An example is Blue Mound, a road connecting Milwaukee with the heart of the western suburbs. That is the fastest-growing 'Magnificent Mile' of Milwaukee, and that is all white. It has superseded downtown as the cultural and business center and is luring the executive buildings and offices. There is a great resistance to extending the bus system all the way out there, because they don't want . . . to contaminate the area.

"I should say, as an Asian American myself,

that Milwaukee is not so much racially prejudiced as psychologically unprepared to integrate. There is not prejudice, but fear of what this integration is going to do.

"One way this fear plays out is by scapegoating the blacks. There are lots of other ethnic groups who have had less of a problem integrating. When the barometer [of trouble] rises, the black community is in the pressure cooker and becomes a scapegoat for it. That's the pressure point. It is like an earthquake fault line, and for Milwaukee, it lies downtown, where the contrast of black and nonblack is the greatest."

Bedi was asked whether the Dahmer killings and the spinoffs that have rocked the city were racial in nature. In between bites of a Manhattan-style chicken salad sandwich, he answered that while "there is a black-white problem in the community, I don't see the Dahmer situation as a black-white situation. I think he sort of exploded the fault line. Part of why he was attracted to where he was, and to his victims, had to do with the dynamics of the community. This is a psychological viewpoint and I have no statistics or data to bear it out, but as a psychiatrist, I take the pulse of this community.

"I think that when there is madness in the community, it always erupts in its mentally ill. They show up the psychology of a system, and its fault lines, and erupt at those weak points. If the Dahmer situation, which happened on a black-white issue, had happened in Chicago, it would not have erupted as much, because Chicago has a better track record of integration. The reason that it caught on so much here is because, in Milwaukee, the situation attached itself to a body of underlying, festering problems. The two problems are in synch, and that made this a fuel-and-fire situation. If the same identical issue had happened elsewhere, it would not have caused the same local and national frenzy."

The lunch time conversation continued:

Question: When Dahmer came here, he had already killed once before and he duplicated that pattern. When he went on his rampage, the black and gay communities seemed to be fertile ground on which he could find victims. How did Jeffrey Dahmer, a white man, work so smoothly with gays and minorities?

Answer: Both of these subgroups are looking for an "affiliation" and that was part of his seduction. He exploited those subgroups in society which were susceptible to having their needs frustrated by the community. They are very prone to abandonment and whenever they get any glimmer of acceptance or recognition, they are susceptible to being seduced into even a bad or dysfunctional relationship.

Look at it from three angles—from the victim's dynamics; the dynamics of the sick person, in this case the criminal; and the dynamics of the system, or community. For a potential problem to become real, certain things have to coalesce, and when each party to the dynamic makes its contribution, then we have a ball game.

For the systems issue, Milwaukee is in the middle of educating itself about racial relationships and integration in its truest sense. There have been European communities that have integrated well—the Italians, Irish, Germans and Jews. Now the second wave of integration is under way. In some ways, Milwaukee is also a "fault line" for the rest of America. The problems you see in Middle America and Milwaukee at present are what the rest of the nation will be facing in the next fifteen to twenty years. For once, we are ahead of California.

The illusion of openness here is a very schizophrenic thing. Milwaukee has a liberal Democratic [tradition], and Wisconsin is a liberal state. That presents a paradox. Milwaukee is as Democratic in tradition and liberal in attitude as it can get, yet there exists this core of racial disharmony, racial insensitivity or unawareness, which is also symbolic of America today.

If you look at any nation in the world you will see such conflicts, be it Hindus and Muslims in India, or the integration problems I've seen in England. America is as liberal and open as any place on the earth can be. But America is grappling with the latest wave of minorities, Laotian and other Asian and others. In places like Milwaukee, in the relative calm and tranquillity of a place like this, you can see these problems erupt.

Question: Where does Dahmer fit into such a mix?

Answer: A psychodynamic assessment of where he is at: We have a person who started out with sexual abuse, alleged, at age eight. His parents had a very bitter divorce when he was eighteen. It looks, not uncommonly, like his parents were just keeping it together until he was eighteen. He lives with his mother for a while, but she takes the younger son someplace and he [Jeffrey] is abandoned once again.

There is some evidence of cruelty to animals, and we find him melting animal bones and things. Then he tends to resolve this disaffiliation by joining the army. People who join the army do it for a number of reasons. People who volunteer, with his profile, mainly do it because they want a sense of connectiveness with fellow human beings. They want some kind of . . . parenting. He joins the army, has a drinking problem, and then he gets kicked out and does not get his affiliative needs met. I am not proposing that this is their fault for not helping him. . . . [H]e was looking for parenting and brotherhood, and somehow it fell through. In his view, his parents abandoned him and now the whole U.S. Army abandoned him. All of the might of the federal government and the U.S. Army could not get him some kind of help. I'm sure they offered, but it is one thing to offer and another to somehow intervene. I think 90 percent of the time, good corporations don't let go of their employees just because of a drinking problem. They somehow help them back into a productive life. I'm not sure how much of that occurred in the army. There it was "shape up or ship out."

After that, we have his problems with sexually abusing children, alcohol addiction and sexual addiction and how the system dealt with him. It was not punitively. They gave him probation and did ask him to get help. But it was not a therapeutic experience, so once again he felt abandoned by the system in that it was more custodial, not therapeutic.

Then there is the "latchkey" phenomenon. "Your father's going to work, I'm going to work, this is the Nintendo box and the Nintendo games and this is the program at four o'clock for you to watch when you come home. There is a sandwich in the microwave oven. You warm it up, watch your Nintendo games and here is the latchkey." The system responded to him just the way the system responds to many of its children lately, by letting the problem just sit there. Dahmer just sat there, but he obviously didn't want to sit there. So he tended to act out, to get someone to listen and respond.

In psychiatric care, we see more and more people who are narcissistic and borderline. These are people who don't know how to connect with other people, who just don't have the right instruments to make connections with others. In the nineteenth century, we had neurotic people, with too much guilt from excessive parenting. Now we don't get people who are guilty, we get people who are tragic, who are disconnected from the rest of the world. They just don't know how to connect. So marriages break down, relationships break down, there is a lack of loyalty and spirituality. I know that sounds like a Republican slogan, but these are real issues.

Question: But not everyone who suffers through some setbacks becomes a criminal.

Answer: There is a bridge, [a point] when some unfortunate incidents in his life coincided, when potential problems became real problems. The bridge is the psychiatric principle of multideterminism, when a number of factors overlap. In this one, we see there was a lot of fire and there was a lot of fuel. It can come from a number of factors [and with] this guy, name it. Everything that could make a contribution to this problem did make a contribution.

There are two parts to each problem. There is the question of "Are you bad, or are you mad?" There is the problem that this guy was bad ostensibly in his behavior, but we're looking at the context—was there a mad context to it?

Question: Loneliness seemed to be a trigger that would set him off. The divorce, having to leave school and home, all seemed to represent a maximum of loneliness and that was when he decided to kill for the first time, to jack up the stakes from animal experimentation to human beings.

Answer: The situation was with his being visible. Take that Honor Society class picture. He jumped into the photo and they blacked out his picture, so he truly was an Invisible Man. I understand his IQ could be in the genius range of 130 to 140, and some people have said his IQ must be more than 120, pending formal assessment. A weird genius. His IQ was good and he had obvious potential and he obviously wanted to be a part of the Honor Society. He did not jump into the picture for the other groups. It was important to him. He wanted to be something his parents could be proud of, something they could look up to, and he was unsuccessful in his attempt. My guess would be it was a major humiliation for him to be blacked out. I wonder why they didn't just take another picture. It was almost set up to humiliate him. That day, he must have made a decision that "no more are people going to black my face out." And now his picture is in the headlines of every major newspaper and magazine in this world. No one is blacking his face out anymore. The *New York Times, People* magazine, CBS. That's the magic comeback.

Question: But killing was not enough. He became sadistic. Why did he go that extra step?

Answer: We all have two forces—sexuality and aggression—and they are a very healthy part of each one of us. We usually metabolize that and digest it in a way that is useful to us and to society. Sexuality, tamed, can become a good nucleus for marriage, intimacy, having children, being tender, gentle, loving, and caring. Aggression helped people who hunted, and help now in protecting your boundaries and aggressively, assertively and joyfully taming new frontiers of life, and protecting yourself, your community, your family, and your children. Both are very useful attributes if they are managed correctly. If they are not, then a number of things happen and they can come out in destructive ways. People who have trouble with sexuality and interpersonal intimacy can only express themselves through aggression.

So when they have a sexual attraction for someone, they can only express it as aggression. They show their love by aggression. They start becoming sadistic. "I want to connect with you, I don't know how to make love to you. I don't know how to be friends with you, but I do know how to be hurtful to you, and I'm going to use the only bridge I have."

You can see, on the outside, how he is calm and tender looking and gentle. Somebody you wouldn't mind sitting down with and having a cup of coffee. I am sure he is intelligent and charming.

The second part is he didn't have any object relations of how to communicate with women. Part of it is possibly his relationship with his mother. If you notice, when the frenzy of killing occurred, [according to Dahmer] there had been no contact between them for five years, and then they reconnect [through the telephone call]. After the call in March, there are seven or eight murders. It seems the bulk of his aggression took place after his mother's call. It was almost as if he had finally managed to secure her attention and he didn't want to lose it again. By doing what he has done, he has irreversibly connected their fates.

Question: What about his homosexuality?

Answer: He does not fit the profile of homosexuals. They are like heterosexuals. They make a choice, and they are joyful about it, not destructive or defensive. His is what I call a defensive homosexuality. It's a retreat to homosexuality because these men or women have not evolved the art to connect with heterosexual encounters and reach across the sexual lines. So they connect with a group that will respond to them promptly. So his choice of victims was because of a number of reasons. He may have had difficulty in connecting with white males. That would have taken more effort on his part, more tact, and he did not have those affiliative skills. So he found it easier to deal with people of color.

Secondly, he felt so inferior, there was a process of identification with the victims. He saw himself as bad and undesirable, disenfranchised and at the bottom of the totem pole. Part of him felt like his victims—bad, black, inferior, at least in his perception. I don't believe blacks are bad, but it was part of his system of looking at it.

At the same time, he wanted to psychologically rid himself of this part of himself. It was bad and ugly and undesirable and disallowed. He did that by first connecting with them, and then cutting them out from his existence. It was not only to make love to them, but to kill them, destroy them and mutilate them, so they do not come back to life.

This is what I call a psychic waste level, these [deaths] were like radioactive psychic waste products. Sexually confused relationships are a very common criterion for borderline individuals. They project part of themselves onto their victims and then try to destroy the victim in order to destroy that part of themselves that they are uncomfortable with. That is why it was almost essential for him to, from his perspective, completely mutilate and destroy. He had to get them [his victims] out of his psychological life.

Question: Then he went the opposite direction and kept their skulls around.

Answer: That is the trophy phenomenon. Most of these people have no visible success. Most of us have our businesses, our children, our other successes, and athletes have trophies of their success. But these people are so disenfranchised that they have no visible trophies. The only trophies he could collect were parts of his victims . . . his only visible symbol of having had any meaning to his own existence. It was so crucial for him to preserve them, protect them, paint them, look after them, and hang on to them.

The other crucial part is that most of these people want to get caught, to fulfill their affiliation needs, so they will leave such visible symbols.

In this case, the symbols were there for years. Even recently, there was this strange aroma from his apartment, photographs and body parts.

Question: Did he know that somebody was going to come in eventually and discover them?

Answer: He had a strong wish that someone would come in and be part of it. He kept attracting people to come in and see his trophies. It was almost like saying, "Please catch me and note that I exist." But people wouldn't, so he kept doing more and more, until he would be observed.

Question: Would he have ever stopped?

Answer: No. Not until he was caught. He had given indications to police, to neighbors, to probation officers, to the United States government, to his parents, and even to his victims that "I am here." He was giving very clear signals that he wanted to be noticed, but people kept denying that.

Question: What about Dahmer having sex with the corpses? Was there a difference in what he was thinking while he was committing those various acts?

Answer: His personality disorder, the alcohol addiction, the pedophilia, the necrophilia, his ego and homosexuality, all were layers of his dysfunction. The preoccupation of having sex with the dead person had to do with his feelings at different points in time.

A living person could not fill his need. Only a dead person, where he was totally in control and there was no way of retaliation, belittlement, ne-

gation, or abandonment. It was not so much being sadistic as wanting to be in control. Then it
became a question of what he is looking for—
nurturing, wanting to be fed, that sort of thing.
If there was a need to show anger, then he might
use anal sex. It depended on what his needs were
in his head at the moment. They could change
quickly as his mood state changed.

Question: There has been a lot of finger pointing as to who is to blame for not stopping him
sooner.

Answer: If there is a silver lining from this
cloud, it is to learn from the whole thing. We have
two choices as a community: we can judge or we
can understand. I'm sure there are the right
channels available to judge him, but for the rest
of us, it will be more beneficial if we can understand the meaning of this.

We can prevent this in bigger or smaller ways.
I submit that in human nature we cannot always
prevent this, for there will always be a dark side
of human nature. It is a prerequisite of human
growth and adaptation. The dark side is the motivation for us to master and grow with it, man-
aging it the best you can. There will always be
mass murderers. There will always be people who
trespass on the rights of others. If we can grow
in civilization, we can put instruments together
to tame the dark side and keep it in check.

We have [communication] satellites, and can
reach Europe, England, Australia by direct dial
in less than five seconds. Yet, the paradox of such

a technologically connected society is that we are disconnected as people.

Question: Why did the nation become so fascinated with this case?

Answer: Because the whole dynamic of this case is also the dynamic of America at this time. Look at the issues that this case is touching on, not the mass murder, but the issues of racial integration, of health and mental health, child care and child rearing, the high divorce rate. It touches the dark side of society, the disconnection that people have. It touches violence and aggression. That is the fascination. Dahmer is merely the smoke. The fire has to do with the issues. Every issue that is burning hot in America is addressed in this case. If we don't heed it, at some point we will think of Jeffrey Dahmer as a tame situation. It is a very gruesome kind of scenario. Like, if you think Three Mile Island was bad, think of Chernobyl.

Question: Could intervention, at any point along the line, have changed Jeffrey Dahmer, or had too many things happened to him for him to settle down?

Answer: He had too many points against him. Any one intervention point could not have stopped him completely. But if intervention had been made, we might have seen much amelioration in the presentation. He may have been a small-time child molester, and that might have gotten him into aggressive treatment and he could have been contained. As an alcoholic, he might have gotten into a recovery mode. But we missed those opportunities. We would have seen a much milder picture if we had been able to intervene in time.

Question: He managed to hold a decent job for six years. Did he become a Jekyll and Hyde, able to turn on charm and put up a sane front at will?

Answer: He is the kind of person we see as a modern psychiatric casualty. In the past, we saw people with a mask of insanity, neurotics who could function well as mature human beings. Now it is reversed. We see people with masks of sanity. They look very sane and normal and charming and adaptive and can rise to echelons of power and prestige in the communities, but they are very sick and very crumbly and fragile and brittle on the inside. These are the people who destroy their workers, their children, and their families. The only difference [between] Jeffrey Dahmer and some of the others is that he used a knife and they destroy people around them emotionally. These people need long-term therapy to heal the inside, to firm up. We just do not have the structure and resources.

Are we going to get organized as people, as a family, as a nation [and] finally have a look and say, finally, "Let's get our house in order"? We are climbing to the moon and stars, but let's come back home and sit down and talk to each other and get organized. Put some systems together so our children can grow in a psychologically detoxified and safe environment.

One thing that intrigues me as a psychiatrist is how much inner capacity we have to heal at any stage. It's never too late. Like plants that are dormant, but come the sunshine of spring and they all come alive and colorful. That's how human nature is. It looks wilted, but give it a little sunshine and a little moisture and the right conditions, and you would be surprised how it flourishes. You don't need any magic. Nature does its own job.

Question: Why do we seem to be producing more mass murderers than the rest of the world?

Answer: A tornado is a good analogy. That is when two divergent masses of air collide with each other. When there is a collision of cultures, when you are at the cutting edge of social and cultural change, you will see these phenomena because there is such a massive shift in the cultural milieu. Jack the Ripper came along when Britain was at the leading edge of such cultural diversity and change. Now we are the pioneers and the standard-bearers and the flagship of the new world order. We are where the cultures collide. It's inevitable. We are it for this age.

CHAPTER TWENTY-TWO

The World of Jeffrey Dahmer

The whole thing was a house of mirrors. Little was what it seemed to be; false reflections were everywhere, and a turn could lead either to a safe exit, into another maze, or you might bump into something that was not quite real, coming the other way.

Bath Township is supposed to be an idyllic place, a small island of tranquillity on the outskirts of the Akron metropolis. In reality, it has been home to several major crimes. Jeffrey Dahmer's slaughter of Steven Hicks was followed only a few years later by a bizarre murder-for-hire case in which an executive was killed in a feud over who was going to take over a business. Summit County Prosecutor Lynn Slaby was elected to office on November 4, 1981, and the very next morning got a call from the sheriff, saying something peculiar had happened up in Bath Township. By the time the complex case was done, eleven people were indicted and eleven were convicted.

Milwaukee had the reputation of being a city where everybody got along together, where people mixed without much regard to color and ethnic background, where German cordiality and the welcoming, *gemütlich* spirit prevailed. The image was badly tarnished in the aftermath of the Dahmer affair, when deep racial divisions came to the surface and serious problems came to light, particularly the lack of confidence that the police had in their chief, and a similar lack of trust that the minority communities had for the law enforcement officers.

Mayor John Norquist, chief executive of the city at the young age of forty, was cruising to reelection the following year, only to see the leadership of the city by his administration suddenly brought into question. He said that the way others, outsiders, viewed Milwaukee was not as important as seeing his administration restore the faith of the various communities. Even while he made that statement, the power structure of the city went into damage-control mode.

Police officers are supposed to be people who can be trusted to make the correct decisions in moments of maximum stress, for that is how they are trained. But around midnight on May 27, three officers failed to make a simple background check on a naked boy and a smooth-talking white man. Their choice to leave the two alone resulted in the death of the boy and allowed the white man to remain free to kill again. The cops then worsened the situation by laughing about their investigation, and their strange brand of humor was recorded on tape for all the world to hear. The entire police force then shot itself in the foot by turning the suspension of the three cops into a major political issue that gave the Milwaukee Police Department the peculiar stance of justifying the fatal decision that signed the death warrant of Konerak Sinthasomphone. Their anger at what has happened says that they still believe cops can do no wrong, for seldom have their leaders expressed sorrow for the deaths that followed the botched investigation.

And, most of all, there is Jeffrey Dahmer, who was not at all what he seemed to be. To seventeen young men and boys, he appeared to be an okay guy with a bankroll big enough to persuade them to come back to his apartment for a session of nude photography. "I can understand how people fell for his stories," said Celeste Dalton, a relative of victim Anthony Sears. "He just doesn't look like the kind of person that would commit the crimes that he did." Once in his clutches, few would escape. For behind the door of apartment

213 in the Oxford Apartments lay not just a one-bedroom flat, but a dungeon, a maw of death.

Then there were Dahmer's allegations of the multiple deaths, the brutalization of the victims, the necrophilia, the pedophilia and the stashing away of human meat to eat. That tale of horror was closely followed by a statement that he did not kill anyone, anywhere, other than the one victim in Ohio and the sixteen others in Wisconsin. Once under the wing of a lawyer, the terminology of the statement reduced the foulness of murder to merely an "incident" or, as attorney Gerald Boyle would say, "these very, very sad things." In other statements, Boyle said Dahmer was feeling remorseful and was overcome with despair and anguish. Authorities in other states were expressing extreme reluctance to believe anything Jeffrey Dahmer had to say, particularly when he had gone through a thorough probationary supervision process without giving so much as a hint that he was slaughtering people, sometimes within hours of talking with his probation officer.

The probationary experience was another of the unreal points of the story, for in theory, a person under maximum supervision is actually being handled. Had a probation agent ever gone to apartment 213 in the "bad neighborhood," he or she would likely have noticed something was not quite right—perhaps a body in the bedroom, or skulls in the closet, or bones in a vat of acid. But they never left their office, as far as Dahmer was concerned.

The Wisconsin Department of Corrections shifted into damage control with the smoothness of a true bureaucracy, ordering agent Donna Chester not to speak to any reporters. All communications were to be handled out of departmental headquarters in Madison, where officials insisted that their department workers could sleep well, because they had followed all the rules in the Jeffrey Dahmer situation.

"As far as the probation or parole agents are concerned, they did exactly what they were required to do under the administrative code, they violated no work rule, they violated no administrative code, they violated no laws. Their actions are perfectly in accordance with our policies and procedures," declared Joseph Scislowicz, the departmental information officer.

He said that Chester was also handling 120 other cases at the same time that she was dealing with Dahmer, and that her supervisor had granted a waiver, relieving her of having to visit his home. "She was not required to go there," said the spokesman, "because of her very heavy caseload."

Even had she or another agent gone to see Dahmer, it was only "speculative" that anything would have been noticed, said Scislowicz. "She did what she was required to do, did a good job, and is a very fine agent." It is true that an agent might not have found anything at the apartment had one gone there, but by staying away, the agents of course would find nothing.

The public information officer, putting his department on the high moral ground, observed, "So many people want to flagellate themselves over this bizarre character. I guess that is their privilege, but we're not going to do it. We're not pointing fingers at anybody." But he added that, if one wanted to speculate, you would have to put Dahmer's neighbors, the police, his counselors, his high school English teacher, his grandmother, his parents, members of the gay community, schoolmates, and the mailman on a list of people who might have prevented the tragedy. He did not list the probationary system that had marked Dahmer down for maximum supervision. "Hindsight is always forty-forty," he said, closing his interview with an appropriately out-of-focus statement.

The public relations man said that the department may ask its various regions to determine how many waivers they are granting on such things as visits to the residences of probationers.

In fact, Scislowicz was correct, to a point. Dahmer certainly hoisted enough storm warnings along the way for someone to have figured out that at least something was seriously wrong with him, all the way back to when he was shooting the breeze with a teenage friend, confiding that he would like to test his taxidermy skills on something more than the usual squirrel. Something, perhaps, like a human being. But in the end, it was the legal system that was to blame, because they are the professionals whose salaries are paid by the taxpayers whom they are to safeguard. With the job comes responsibility to take an extra step whenever necessary, to run the identification checks and to follow up when report after report turns up on a probation officer's desk stating that someone under maximum supervision is going downhill. In Milwaukee, those public servants took the easy way out, with disastrous consequences.

At the end, comedic things began to happen. Two city cops on the suicide watch in Dahmer's cell reportedly obtained his autograph.

Authorities had a difficult time piecing together the concoction that Dahmer used as a sleeping potion, but early on they began to focus on benzodiazepine, a tranquilizing prescription medication that he could have received while under treatment as part of his probationary status. Other drugs that were being discovered in victims' tissues by the medical examiner were Halcion, cocaine, and a type of menzodiazepine, while searchers in the apartment picked up a prescription for Lorazepam, another form of benzodiazepine. Such drugs have a strong effect when mixed with alcohol, and in quantity could probably, experts say, render someone unconscious. Chloroform had been found in Dahmer's closet.

After his victims had passed out and been killed

by strangulation, Dahmer then faced a monumental task. Every time he found himself with a new corpse in his tiny apartment, he had to dispose of the body. That would not be an easy job at any time but particularly when you live in the middle of a city, surrounded by people on all sides.

For starters, it is very messy. An average American male body contains about thirteen pints of blood. The arithmetic is easy, because two pints equal one quart, and four quarts equal one gallon. But to put the volume into context, consider this as an example:

Suppose you go to the dairy case in your local supermarket, and into your basket you load one big gallon jug of milk, one tall quart of orange juice, and a little pint carton of cottage cheese. Now suppose that instead of the milk, o.j., and cottage cheese, each of the containers in your cart were filled instead with blood. That is about the amount of blood that Jeffrey Dahmer had to get rid of every time he began to butcher a body. And he claims to have done it seventeen times.

Smaller people would have meant less blood, of course, but the rule of thumb is about a pint of blood for every twelve pounds of body weight. It would be a formidable task to wash away that much blood, since it is about three times thicker than water. Complicating even that task would be the fact that it would be combined with the other bodily fluids present at death.

Then he had to deal with the various organs.

Once the heart stops beating about four times per breath, it becomes just a lump about as big as a fist and weighing just under a pound. Then there is the stomach, that J-shaped receptacle that takes up space in the middle of the torso, up to thirty feet of intestines, and a brain weighing about three mushy pounds.

It is not easy to dispose of a human body.

There are 656 muscles, tight sinews, some more than a foot in length, that are strong and so fibrous that they resist all but the sharpest knife.

But muscles are relatively soft, unlike the 206 bones in a body, a multitude of big and little obstacles to a saw. Each arm has 32 bones and a leg has 31. The skull, which many people think of as a single thing, actually is made up of 29 different bones. The spine has 26, there are 6 in both ears, and even 1 in the throat.

And the hardest of all are the enamel and dentine that make up a tooth. Archaeologists regularly uncover teeth that have been buried for thousands of years. In addition, the thirty-two permanent teeth of an adult human is like a roadmap to his or her identity. Comparing dental records is an accepted method of determining the name of a John Doe in the morgue.

So, seventeen times Dahmer faced this daunting task. With the help of modern power tools and technology, a bathtub, some plastic garbage bags, and the unwitting assistance of neighbors who didn't pursue their questions about the smells of decay and odd noises coming from Dahmer's apartment, he was able to carry off the deed, time after time. Crushing bones, draining away blood, using a barrel of acid to pull away stubborn flesh and simply tossing the scraps, wrapped in plastic bags, onto the garbage heap. He was able to do it not just once, but seventeen times, disposing of most of the evidence, except for the skulls he kept as trophies and various body segments that he refrigerated, according to his own words, to eat at his convenience.

Perhaps the single most important influence on Dahmer's life, on a continuing basis, was alcohol. Classmates report that by the seventh grade, just out of grammar school in Bath Township, he would come to school reeking of alcohol. In later years, he would wear a long coat into class, with a flask or bottle of whiskey tucked securely in an inside pocket. On breaks, while some boys might sneak into the restroom to try a cigarette, Dahmer would find some private corner and have a drink or two. Fifteen years ago, when Dahmer was coasting through the public school system, the idea of a teenager being an alcoholic was a foreign concept. Today, we know better. Most alcoholics start when they are very young, getting someone to buy a six-pack for them, or drinking from their parents' private stock, or even sharing a brew with Dad while a football game is on television.

By the time he hit college and the army, he was

a full-fledged alcoholic, unable to get through the day without drawing some courage from a bottle. Nothing emphasized that disease as much as the episodes of wildness that marked his behavior when he returned to Ohio from the army. The signals were all there. At one point, he apparently went to a few meetings of Alcoholics Anonymous, but the simple truth that would have been espoused there—that Jeffrey Dahmer alone was responsible for Jeffrey Dahmer—would not have been what he wanted to hear. He was not ready to put the bottle down. His morose drinking eventually cost him everything—his job, his friends and even his freedom. But it was also a prime factor in costing seventeen people their lives.

An interesting point is that not only were the scientific profiles of a serial killer right on the money with Jeffrey Dahmer, but so would be an astrological reading for this Gemini, who was born under the sign of the twins, the two different personalities in one person. Not all Geminis, of course, tend toward criminal behavior, for that particular sign of the zodiac has produced such creative people as Walt Whitman, Ralph Waldo Emerson, and Thomas Mann. But a reading of his chart would have shown the following, for those who follow such things.

Dahmer was born on the Taurus cusp, with his moon in Aries, and of "his" planets, an astrologer would find Mercury in Gemini, Venus in Taurus, Mars in Aries, Jupiter and Saturn in Capricorn,

Uranus in Leo, Neptune in Scorpio. The sun would be in Gemini, giving him an urge to be different, a rule-breaker who rebels against authority, but ready and glib in his speech. The moon in Aries would mean he possessed a flaring anger and longed for power. He would be a restless, hotheaded, and dangerous opponent who enjoys a stalking hunt.

Other "planetary" attributes would be a love to touch and possess people, holding on to them tightly. He would play to win and take a loss personally, have a large sexual ego, and like to play the conqueror. A melancholy, suspicious personality would dominate him. And, with his Neptune in Scorpio, the astrologer would find that such a person has a love for chemistry, with a possible addiction to alcohol.

CHAPTER TWENTY-THREE

Trial

The Jeffrey Dahmer case was not over with his arrest, nor with his 179-page confession. The furore that had gripped Milwaukee quieted as autumn passed into winter, although things continued to stir. Disciplinary proceedings were pressed against the policemen who returned Konerak Sinthasomphone to Dahmer: officers John Balcerzak and Joseph Gabrish were fired, while officer Richard Porubcan was placed on a year's probationary status—decisions that were immediately appealed.

On January 13, 1992, with the dawning of the New Year, Dahmer reclaimed the headlines. In a surprise decision that went against the advice of his lawyer, Dahmer discarded his innocent plea and told the court he was guilty, but that he was insane.

The declaration turned the case on its head. Now, instead of having to prove his man did not commit the murders, defense attorney Gerald Boyle would unroll one of the goriest tapestries ever seen in an American courtroom. His task was to convince a twelve-person jury that Dahmer was crazy, because only an insane person would do the things he did.

Two weeks later, on January 27, Dahmer was back in the spotlight, as a winter snowstorm cleared and all eyes turned to the fifth-floor courtroom of Judge Laurence C. Gram, Jr. The world would soon learn what had really happened in that little flat of horrors.

The queue began before dawn to claim the handful of hard, fold-down courtroom seats not reserved for the media or the families of Dahmer's victims. Groupies who devoured every word about Dahmer showed up, as did law students, curious passers-by and even a rap music neophyte who had written a ditty about the crimes. In the courtroom, a wall of plexiglass separated the audience from the trial area. Among those in attendance each day were Lionel and Shari Dahmer, Jeffrey's father and stepmother, who would sit quietly together, holding hands, faces frozen in neutral.

A jury of a dozen citizens had to be picked from a 150-name list. "You're going to hear about things you probably didn't know existed in the real world," Boyle warned. "In this case, you're going to hear about sexual conduct before death, during death and after death. Will you be so disgusted by that you won't be able to listen?"

Timid hands were raised and the size of the jury pool shrunk. They were told they would be sequestered away from their homes and families, under guard, during the three-week trial. More hands went up. Finally, Boyle, District Attorney McCann and Judge Gram took the remaining pool members into the judge's private chambers for final questioning. Like a couple of farmers, McCann and Boyle picked through the crop, the D.A. weeding out anyone with a bias against homosexuals, while Boyle discarded those who did not like psychiatrists.

One woman was excused because she hand-fed little birds with syringes and the "little darlings" would die without her care. Dahmer smiled at that and made a quiet joke to a policeman. Another potential juror left because he was almost deaf; a woman had to care for an elderly person; a man said his mind was already made up; a woman said she could not cope with this particular case; a man said his brother worked with Jeffrey at the chocolate factory. Finally, a dozen jurors and two alternates were selected—seven men and seven women, ranging in age from twenty to sixty-five, only one of them black. A former secretary, a punch press operator, a nurse, a married man with children, a former soldier and a fashion expert all found places in the jury box.

And so began the trial of the tall, lanky man dressed in an open-neck white shirt, a brown sport coat, tan pants and penny loafers. Each day, Dahmer was so heavily shackled before leaving his cell that deputies would bring him in a wheelchair to a private courtroom entrance. There they would unlock the chains and Dahmer would remove his glasses before he strolled into court.

Boyle had a list of forty-five witnesses, while McCann had ninety-five ready as the lawyers gave their opening arguments. In the coming weeks, Boyle had to prove that Dahmer was insane, while McCann did not have to prove his sanity, only that he knew right from wrong.

Boyle came out swinging, intent on convincing the jurors that Dahmer was a killing machine totally unable to stop himself from butchering human beings.

Nonsense, retaliated McCann. Jeffrey Dahmer was not crazy, just lustful and selfishly feeding his sexual fantasies without concern for the havoc he was causing. Here, according to his version, was a man who, at times, was a functioning member of society, able even to fill in his tax forms on time, hold a steady job and do any number of routine things.

The jury started out confused, and affairs would only get more tangled. Its decision would not have to be unanimous because of the changed plea, but at least ten would have to agree on any verdict reached. There were two parts to each of the fifteen charges before the jurors and they had to first decide whether at the time of each crime, Dahmer possessed a mental disease or defect. If the answer was affirmative, then a second question had to be decided: whether with that defect or disease Dahmer was unable to distinguish right from wrong. "Yes" answers to both questions would send Dahmer to a mental institution. "No" answers would send him to a state prison.

The defense attorney wasted no time in horrifying the jury with new information. From the age of fourteen his client daydreamed of having sex with dead bodies, the baseline that Boyle wanted to establish for the disease of necrophilia. At fifteen, Dahmer was obsessed with a jogger who trotted past his home every day in Bath, Ohio. He wanted to kill the man and have sex with the corpse. Young Dahmer sawed off a baseball bat, took his bicycle and went out to search for the runner. Inexplicably, he never saw the man again.

When he wanted to kill a hitchhiker, the unfortunate Stephen Hicks fitted the bill. Once Hicks was dead, Dahmer masturbated on the body, then sliced it open two days later to "see what it looked like on the inside."

With the horror show in full stride, the eyes of the jurors almost glazed over in shock. Cannibalism, Boyle added, eventually evolved. "He ate body parts . . . so that these poor people he killed would become alive again in him," declared Boyle.

The lawyer then described how Dahmer performed experimental surgery on some of his unconscious victims, drilling holes in their heads while they were still alive and pouring acid into their wounds. Why? "He wanted to create zombies, people who would be there for him."

Oh, yes, Boyle said, remember when Jeffrey was serving his ten months in jail during the day and working nights at the chocolate factory? Well, he stashed body parts in his locker at the food plant so he could play with them at work and relive his experiences.

Boyle asked the jury, "Was he evil or was he sick?" If the vote could have been taken then, there would probably have been a unanimous declaration that Dahmer was as crazy as any man had ever been.

McCann was quick to respond, telling the jury to brush everything Boyle had said right off the table. Jeffrey Dahmer, according to the D.A., was a master manipulator and deceiver who knew exactly what he was doing every step of the way, able to turn his urges on and off as easily as flipping a light switch. Did he attack other soldiers while he was in the army? Other students while at Ohio State University? Did he hear little voices in his head? No, insisted McCann, he didn't.

The deaths, he said, were not the acts of a madman, but the result of meticulous planning.

"Dahmer knew it was wrong," said McCann. "He was a person who wanted something and wasn't going to take 'no' for an answer."

McCann brought on the detectives who sat with Dahmer through sixty hours of confession. They claimed the defendant was well aware of his actions.

"He felt a tremendous amount of guilt because of his actions. He felt thoroughly evil," said Detective Dennis Murphy. He read Dahmer's own words: "It's hard for me to believe that a human being could have done what I've done, but I know that I did it."

Dahmer's confession stated his emotions were mixed while he dismembered his victims; the fear of being caught was overwhelmed by the excitement of being in total control. The flesh was distributed in three-ply plastic trash bags, no more than twenty-five pounds per bag, and thrown into rubbish bins—he always took his clothes off before doing this, because the job was "quite messy". Dahmer plopped the bones into an acid solution until they became mushy enough to be flushed down the toilet.

Dahmer told police he kept the skulls because they "represented the true essence of his victims," but insisted that his acts were not racially motivated, claiming his victims were chosen simply because they fit physical criteria. Dahmer preferred his victims to be slim, about medium height with smooth skin. "Race, creed and color had nothing to do with it. It was the opportunity and whoever accepted his offer," Murphy testified.

The serial killer himself became a victim of a freak on Thanksgiving Day of 1989, while still serving his jail sentence. On a holiday pass, after dining at his grandmother's home, Dahmer got drunk and, on a troll of the 219 Club, he met a white man with long, dark hair and a beard. Dahmer passed out in the man's apartment and awoke to find himself hanging from hooks in the ceiling, his legs bound together and his arms tied behind his back, while the man sexually assaulted Dahmer's anus with a candle. Dahmer, who had killed and butchered so many without pity, screamed until he was set free.

"He stated he chalked this up as an experience he had to incur because of his high-risk lifestyle. He stated that this time he was the victim," Murphy said.

Deeply hidden thoughts surfaced in Dahmer's confession. He blamed himself for the anger between his parents and said he felt his mother never recovered from the postpartum depression after he was born. He described everything in matter-of-fact tones, never once crying. Not for his victims, or for himself.

When he was fired from his job and his killing sprees increased, Dahmer thought about turning his life around, getting another job, throwing away his collection of bodies and bones, and starting again. But he realized that probably would never happen. "If I am to be honest with myself, I would have to admit that if I again was set up in another apartment and had the opportunity, I probably would not be able to stop. I feel it is almost a driving compulsion to commit these acts, and I probably would have started up again after some time."

His confession read like a menu of the bizarre.

• While in high school, where his life "revolved totally around smoking pot," he and a friend would drive around, trying to hit dogs, once smashing six in one day. He recalled a crushed beagle hound tumbling over the top of the speeding vehicle. "I've never seen such a look of terror in an animal's eyes. It was sickening."

• Dahmer had an offer of marriage from a woman, whose name he thought was Julie, in Miami. She was from England and had long, curly black hair. An illegal alien in the United States, she could be a permanent resident if her friend Jeffrey would marry her, she explained during their walks on Florida's sandy beaches and over an occasional dinner. Dahmer turned her down because he did not find her physically attractive.

• He chopped up the three men he killed at his grandmother's home while she was at church, disposing of one of them on Easter Sunday. He even attended church with her occasionally.

• Before going out on a hunt, Dahmer would grind up sleeping pills and put the powder in a glass, to which he would later add coffee or alcohol to make the knock-out potion.

Murphy was asked if Dahmer ever showed signs of delusions, if he was "ever out of touch with reality." No, the policeman replied.

Instead, it was his opinion that Dahmer's confidence grew as time passed and that he was adept at bluffing his way through any jam or kill without being detected. Dahmer even praised the officers who were disciplined for their investigation of the Konerak affair, saying they did everything that could have been expected of them. "He took pleasure in the fact of knowing that he had a private world of his own that no one else knew about. He felt he had this ability to make people see a face of him that he wished them to see, and this encouraged him to continue with his crimes, feeling that he would never get caught."

The testimony of Tracy Edwards, whose narrow escape brought Jeffrey Dahmer's secret world crashing down, had a mixed effect on the jury. Boyle used Edwards to show that Dahmer could be friendly or ferocious, talkative or taunting. Edwards, who had enjoyed his time in the limelight being sought out by sensationalist television shows like *Geraldo,* obliged. He said that while watching horror videos on TV, Dahmer started a low, chanting moan, rocking back and forth. "It was like it wasn't him anymore. It was like it was a totally different guy there," Edwards said.

McCann wasn't buying it. He set out to show that Edwards' answers in court didn't correspond to what he said on the television shows. Edwards claimed there were eight locks on the door and McCann proved there were only two. Did he or did he not see a head and hand in the apartment, because he had said both? McCann scolded. "I try to block things like that out," a chagrined Edwards replied. By showing the exaggerations, McCann diluted potentially damaging testimony almost to a point of irrelevance.

It finally came down to a contest between the psychiatrists hired by the defense, the prosecution and the court itself. Their expertise and explanations of obscure medical terminology would be the basis on which the jurors would determine whether Dahmer was insane, in the legal context of the word. But even their testimony was gruesome, including one report that Dahmer had planned to build a "temple" in his little apartment. He sketched it out: a long black table with a line of ten skulls, flanked by full skeletons at each end, with a black chair in which he could sit and stare at the trophies. The display would stand before blue curtains, and a plaque depicting the head of a goat would hang on the wall. Four overhead blue lights would provide illumination and incense would waft up from the table. The experts said Dahmer wanted it to be a "power centre" that would grant him social and financial success. "It's demonstrative of a bizarre delusion. It has no basis in reality and shows a distortion in his thought process," said Chicago psychiatrist Carl M. Wahlstrom. To limit the impact,

McCann pointed out that the young Wahlstrom had never testified before as an expert before a jury.

Judith V. Becker, a sexual disorders specialist at the University of Arizona Medical Center, insisted Dahmer was not pretending insanity. She branded him a necrophiliac, but stopped short of saying he was psychotic. "He has a mental disease. That is what drives his behavior."

In the legal-medical world, necrophilia is described as a sexual disorder, but this does not mean the sufferer has lost touch with reality. A psychotic disorder is usually accompanied by incoherence and hallucinations. This significant point was emphasized to the jurors, for if Dahmer were shown to be rational in much of his life, he could not, therefore, be psychotic, which would mean he was legally sane.

But every time they started to think he was sane, the befuddled jurors would recall Becker's testimony that Dahmer claimed to have had sex with all seventeen victims after killing them, even cutting open their stomachs to have intercourse with the organs inside. Could a sane person do this?

The main defense psychiatrist was Fred S. Berlin, director of the Sexual Disorders Clinic at the famed Johns Hopkins Hospital in Baltimore. An imposing, gruff man on the stand, Berlin engaged with McCann in several loud exchanges as the district attorney slowly undermined the conclusions of the doctor, who had spent four hours interviewing Dahmer.

Declaring Dahmer to be a necrophiliac "wasn't a tough call. He sure seemed out of control to me," said Berlin. Then he dug his heels in with a comment that rang in the heads of the jurors.

"If this isn't mental illness from my point of view, I don't know what is. Are there going to be doctors who are going to say this isn't mental illness? Maybe, but I think that is a pretty difficult point of view to try to defend."

McCann, however, got Berlin to agree that Dahmer could, when necessary, control himself. He did not kill everyone who entered his apartment and he would go home alone if unable to find a suitable partner. "Certainly he was capable of deferring in the way you've just described," Berlin admitted.

George Palermo, a Milwaukee psychiatrist appointed by the court, said Dahmer suffered from a serious personality disorder which needed treatment. "But, he's not psychotic . . . and he's not legally insane."

Frederick Fosdal, of nearby Madison, was one of two psychiatrists brought in by the prosecution. In contrast to Berlin's four hours with Dahmer, Fosdal had logged 117 hours of interviews. His conclusion: "The disorder explains his motivation and explains his behavior", but this disorder did not cause him to lack "the substantial capacity" to know right from wrong.

In a telling moment, Boyle, after one session,

was asked to estimate the odds of a murderer being declared insane just because of a sexual disorder. "About five trillion to one," he replied.

He tried to put a positive spin on things, however, by pointing out that five psychiatrists agreed with many of his positions. "If I'm a juror, I'm going to wonder about this guy chanting, rocking, praying, eating body parts, and looking at some of the other things that he's done, you know, taking showers with two dead bodies in the bathtub—whether we've got somebody who's got some delusional thinking."

But Boyle's case was rocked the very next day when a nationally known expert on serial killers and sexual disorders, Park Dietz of California, came to the witness stand and convincingly stated that Dahmer knew exactly what he was doing. "There was no force pushing him to kill. There was merely a desire to spend more time with the victim."

Having spent eighteen hours interviewing Dahmer, Dietz testified that he suffered from paraphilia (a term for sexual deviance) and a dependence on alcohol. But he added that in every instance Dahmer knew right from wrong and could have stopped his actions if discovered at an inconvenient moment.

Dahmer would pump himself up before a night out by watching pornographic movies, grinding up the sleeping potion and drinking enough to get the courage to carry out the deed. "All of that is an indication that these behaviors were not impulsive. The killing was never an impulsive act. It was always a planned and deliberated act," said Dietz.

As further evidence that Dahmer thought matters through, Dietz reported that the man on trial always used condoms when having sex with a corpse. Dahmer's schemes also indicated that his behavior was not impulsive. For example, he would freeze the corpse of a special victim so he could have repeated sexual encounters with it, or turn someone into a compliant zombie by linking a homemade electrical device into the brain and plugging a power cord into a wall socket.

In his closing summation, Boyle itemized the dirty laundry list of Jeffrey Dahmer's actions, asking if someone could be sane who had tried to have sex with a department store dummy, or hung around graveyards in hopes of digging up a body to satisfy his urges, or masturbating on a filleted corpse. He said his client was like "a runaway train on a track of madness, picking up steam all the time, on and on and on. And it was only going to stop when he hit a concrete barrier or he hit another train. And he hit it, thanks be to God, when Tracy Edwards got the hell out of that room."

McCann was confident that Boyle had fallen perhaps several bricks shy of building the wall of doubt the jurors needed to rule Dahmer insane and let him escape a prison cell. The district attorney described Dahmer simply as a man who killed seventeen people in cold blood to satisfy an extraordinary sexual craving. "Ladies and gentlemen, he's fooled a lot of people. Please, don't let this murderous killer fool you."

The jury's decision came quickly and its verdict, was read to a tense, packed courtroom, with Jeffrey Dahmer sitting straight in his chair, his face an emotionless mask. It was total defeat for the defense. Ten of the twelve jurors, all that was necessary, said Dahmer was not suffering from a mental disease. That meant the right-or-wrong question did not even have to be addressed.

Family members of his victims wept at the verdict. Dahmer merely leaned over to his attorney and whispered, "Thanks for trying."

On the final day of the three-week trial, there was an opportunity for those involved to make statements. Dahmer, wearing his glasses and orange prison coveralls, read slowly from a prepared statement.

"It is over now. This has never been a case of trying to get free. I didn't want freedom. Frankly I wanted death for myself. I knew I was sick or evil or both. I know how much harm I have caused, but I tried to do the best I could after the arrest to make amends. My attempt to identify the remains was the best I could do and that was hardly anything."

The relatives were also allowed to speak, but that exercise was short-lived. Rita Isabell, the oldest sister of Errol Lindsey, began to rave, "Jeffrey Dahmer, I hate you," and lunged toward the convicted man. Deputies grabbed her and Dahmer was quickly led away.

The fifteen consecutive terms of life imprisonment without the possibility of parole to which Dahmer was sentenced on February 15 guaranteed that he would dwell for the rest of his life in a prison cell at Columbia Correctional Institution in Portage, Wisconsin, to be kept alone and under constant watch.

Three months later Dahmer would be found guilty of the murder of Stephen Hicks in Ohio, a state with sanity laws even tougher than Wisconsin, and given a sixteenth life sentence.

Jeffrey Dahmer will never again stalk the streets.

It fell to McCann to sum up, which he did succinctly. "The real tragedy here is I believe he could have stopped at any time. He was not a rolling train. He was the engineer of a rolling train."

CHAPTER TWENTY-FOUR

Death

Following the convictions, Jeffrey Dahmer was taken away to spend the rest of his life at the Columbia Correctional Institute in Portage, Wisconsin, about 75 miles from his killing ground of Milwaukee. The rather gentle name of the red-brick complex of buildings is misleading, because the more than 600 inmates incarcerated there are actually in a maximum-security prison for dangerous men.

Dahmer's new home within that prison was a tiny cell eight feet wide by ten feet long. In a period when America's prisons were notoriously overcrowded, Dahmer lived alone, unable to look forward to his first parole hearing, which would not be until March, 2934, after he had served at least 941 years in prison. Nobody lived that long.

The prison had been awarded America's most notorious serial killer, and a number-one priority was the safety of the man beginning to serve out his 15 life terms for the horrible Milwaukee murders. Dahmer's entire first year in prison was spent in protective isolation, because prison officials worried that some other violent inmate at the CCI, someone perhaps with nothing to lose, would kill him.

Such prison assaults are not new. The man who killed Dahmer would automatically jump from a societal misfit to an asterisk in history—the man who murdered the cannibal killer. The prison warders were determined that such an assassination would not take place.

The plan worked. For a while.

Dahmer's days were carefully planned and monitored. He wore green cotton prison uniforms, read books and magazines (no pornography involving bondage was allowed), ate his meals and let the days roll by.

The first year passed without major incident, much to the pleasure of the Wisconsin authorities, although in March, 1992, guards discovered a small razor blade tucked away in an envelope in his trash can. Dahmer was punished. For a while, he was not allowed to watch television or buy things from the commissary.

Then, incredibly, they seemed to forget Jeffrey

Dahmer's secret—that during his entire life, he could and did become anyone he wanted to be. If he wanted to con a cop, he became the contrite, polite young man. If he wanted to lure a victim home, he became the charming homosexual. Now it was time to become the model prisoner. And he did. The support systems that had believed Dahmer's act and failed to perform their checks and balances throughout his life—the family, schools, college, army, police, courts and probation officers—were about to encounter another final, dismal failure.

There were occasional family visits, and Dahmer started reading his Bible, delving into religion to the extent that he was allowed to be baptized in the prison's whirlpool bath by the Reverend Roy Ratcliffe, who said Dahmer had been forgiven by God.

But Jeffrey Dahmer was bored sitting alone in that cell. After spending months in isolation, he wanted more human contact, even if he had to put up with the taunts of other convicts, sometimes joking with them to leave him alone because "I bite." Certainly his record was relatively clean, since he had been watched closely that first year. In response, the prison officials opened Dahmer's world a little bit, assigning him to a unit that was reserved for inmates with severe emotional problems, allowing him to mix with other prisoners. Supervision was still tight, but not the same as before, automatically elevating the danger level.

To outsiders, the unfolding months brought

surprises that indicated the reins were loosened on the prize prisoner of Portage. He wasn't exactly in the general population, which would probably guarantee certain death at the hands of a fellow prisoner in a state that had gone to great expense at trial not to sentence him to death. However, Dahmer was allowed to mingle with men who were not exactly serving their life terms for jaywalking. Like him, many were murderers, although not in his superstar class.

A clear sign that he was edging into dangerous waters came on July 3, 1994, during a prison chapel service. Another inmate who had honed a toothbrush into a knife tried to slit Dahmer's throat, but only caused a scratch. Instead of seeing the incident as a red flag, the authorities apparently agreed with Dahmer's own interpretation that he was safe. The attacker was a newcomer to the unit, a Cuban who, Dahmer said, had never said a word to him and wanted to get deported by doing something awful. They all brushed off the incident, saying Dahmer was, in bureaucratic terms, "at no undue risk."

Subsequently, things reached a ridiculous stage. After Dahmer's father published a book about his son and their family life, prison authorities actually allowed Jeffrey Dahmer to appear on national television shows. The prisoner appeared, on camera, to be a bit pudgy, but neat, coherent, and contrite, and accepted responsibility for his horrible actions in the outside world.

It was as if the CCI were a kindergarten showing off its prized, well-behaved and intelligent pupil.

Jeffrey Dahmer was already an icon of violence in a violent society, and, to many, his TV appearances showed strange judgment on behalf of the television producers and reporters as well as the prison officials. Instead of an alcoholic nobody who worked at a chocolate factory, Dahmer had entered the realm of legend, and those involved were perpetuating his notoriety. Dahmer was in prison, but America had few prisoners who could match his celebrity, which still seemed to be blossoming three years after his multiple convictions.

Meanwhile, experts involved in the case were shocked and wondering what the hell was going on at the prison, but knowing the answer already. Dahmer had pulled another con job. He had wanted out of the all-day protective security to mix with other inmates, and instead of remembering that he had killed and killed and killed some more, the authorities apparently felt sorry for Dahmer, sitting behind bars in a tiny cell all day. They began to allow him closer contact with other inmates. A time bomb ticking, and nobody at the CCI seemed to hear it. After all, Jeffrey was doing fine in his weekly Bible study, wasn't he? He was a model prisoner, wasn't he? He never caused trouble, did he?

The attack in the chapel already dismissed, Dahmer was now socializing with other inmates in his cellblock, eating his meals in a communal setting—and he even had a job! For an hour and a half every day, he would sweep and mop parts of the prison as part of a team of inmates doing janitorial duty.

As November 1993 began, he was paired with two other men on a clean-up detail. It would have been difficult to match up three more terrifying personalities on a mop-and-pail team than Dahmer, Jesse Anderson and Christopher Scarver. Everyone knew how Dahmer had landed in prison, and it was not an unknown factor that many of the people he had butchered were black. Anderson, a 37-year-old white man, was there for killing his wife in Milwaukee and blaming the murder on a black man, infuriating that city's minority community once again. Scarver, 25 and black, was also serving a life term at Portage for first-degree murder. He was a strong man who was described as delusional, schizophrenic and manic-depressive, and who claimed to be the million-year-old son of God.

At 7:50 A.M. on Monday morning, November 28, after breakfast, the three men were taken by guards to mop the shower and toilet area adjacent to the prison's shiny wood basketball court. As Dahmer set to work cleaning a corner restroom, the guards left the three violent personalities alone with fate.

The guards came back at 8:10 A.M., only twenty minutes later, and found a scene of bloody chaos. Dahmer was discovered facedown and unconscious in a pool of blood, his head crushed. Part of a bloody broom handle was found nearby. The alarm was sounded.

Moments later, the supine body of Jesse Anderson was found some distance away on the tile floor of the shower room, also severely injured. Both were rushed into ambulances and taken to the nearest hospital for treatment of extensive head trauma.

It was in that emergency room that Jeffrey Dahmer was pronounced dead at 9:11 A.M. Paramedics said it appeared that his face and head had been slammed repeatedly against the floor or wall, and compared the injuries to those a person might sustain in a terrible traffic accident. Anderson died a short time later.

The life of Jeffrey Dahmer was finally over, but his legacy was destined to live on, and every subsequent development seemed to perpetuate his horrible history.

Prison officials went into a pretzel-like position. They insisted that guards had followed procedures and nothing had been done incorrectly, while at the same time they launched an investigation to see if Christopher Scarver should be the lone suspect or whether Dahmer had been the target of a conspiracy that may have even included a prison worker.

It didn't really matter. The simple fact was that Jeffrey Dahmer was dead. He had been placed in jeopardy instead of being kept under close supervision. The same mentality that had prevented his probation officers from keeping watch on him had prevailed one last time, again with a terrifying result.

The families of his victims were not unhappy that Dahmer was gone. A lawyer who represented them in getting a rather empty victory of $80 million in compensation from a destitute Dahmer said that an auction of 312 articles he owned, including the refrigerator in which he stored body parts, might bring more money now that the cannibal was dead.

The two police officers who had been dismissed for giving 14-year-old Konerak Sinthasomphone back to Dahmer for slaughter on May 27, 1991, won reinstatement to their jobs after a long court battle, although one resigned a short time later.

The apartment building where Dahmer lived had been razed and a high fence erected around the property, but the tourist shop across the street reported a sudden burst of business upon the news of Dahmer's demise.

As with his victims, the death of Jeffrey Dahmer was not the end of the story. A controversy immediately arose over the disposition of his remains.

Chronology

May 21, 1960 Jeffrey Lionel Dahmer is born in Milwaukee, Wisconsin.

May 17, 1968 Dahmer family moves to 4480 West Bath Road, Bath Township, Ohio.

June 1978 Jeffrey Dahmer graduates from Revere High School.

June 18, 1978 Dahmer picks up hitchhiker Steven Hicks, who becomes Dahmer's first murder victim.

July 24, 1978 Divorce is granted to Lionel and Joyce Dahmer.

Aug. 1978 Joyce Dahmer takes younger son, David, and moves to Chippewa Falls, Wisconsin. Jeffrey is left alone in the house in Bath until his father finds him there and moves back in.

Sept.–Dec. 1978 Jeffrey attends one freshman quarter at Ohio State University in Columbus, Ohio.

Dec. 24, 1978 Lionel Dahmer weds Shari Shinn Jordan.

Dec. 29, 1978 Jeffrey Dahmer starts three-year hitch in U.S. Army, reports for duty Jan. 12, 1979.

July 13, 1979 Dahmer completes training as medical specialist and is assigned duty post in Baumholder, Germany.

Mar. 26, 1981 Dahmer is discharged from the

army in South Carolina because of excessive drinking. He drifts to South Florida.

1982 He moves into the home of his paternal grandmother, Catherine Dahmer, at 2357 South 57th St. in West Allis, Wisconsin.

1982 Dahmer is cited for indecent exposure at the Wisconsin State Fair.

1985 Dahmer is hired as a laborer at the Ambrosia Chocolate Company in Milwaukee.

1986 Dahmer is arrested for urinating in public.

Sept. 15, 1987 Steven W. Tuomi, twenty-eight, of Michigan, disappears. He is not officially reported missing until January 1989. Dahmer identifies him later as a victim.

Jan. 1988 James E. Doxtator, a fourteen-year-old Native American, is picked up by Dahmer, taken to the house in West Allis, and killed.

Mar. 1988 Richard Guerrero meets Dahmer and is killed in the house in West Allis.

1988 Dahmer moves out of his grandmother's house in West Allis and into his own apartment at the Oxford Apartments, 924 North Twenty-fifth Street.

Aug. 1988 Dahmer is arrested for molesting a 13-year-old boy.

Jan. 30, 1989 Dahmer is convicted on charge of sexual assault and enticing a child for immoral purposes.

Mar. 25, 1989 Dahmer picks up Anthony Sears at the LaCage bar and takes him to his grandmother's house and kills him.

May 23, 1989 Dahmer is sentenced to five years' probation. Spends first year in a work-release program in the Milwaukee County House of Corrections.

Mar. 1990 Dahmer is released two months early from work-release program.

June 1990 Edward W. Smith meets Dahmer, is taken to the apartment, drugged and killed.

July 1990 Dahmer meets Raymond Smith a/k/a Ricky Beeks at the 219 Club in Milwaukee, takes him to his apartment, and kills him.

Sept. 3, 1990 Ernest Miller leaves his aunt's home and vanishes. Dahmer later tells police that he met Miller in front of a bookshop on North Twenty-seventh Street in Milwaukee. He takes him to his apartment and kills him.

Sept. 24, 1990 David C. Thomas is reported missing by his girlfriend. Dahmer later says he killed him in the apartment.

Feb. 18, 1991 Curtis Straughter is last seen by his grandmother. Dahmer meets him at a bus stop near Marquette University, takes him to his apartment, and kills him.

April 7, 1991 Errol Lindsey is last seen going to the store by his sister. Dahmer later says he met him on the corner of Twenty-seventh and Kilbourn, took him to his apartment, and killed him.

May 24, 1991 Anthony Hughes, a deaf-mute, meets Dahmer outside the 219 Club on Second Street, goes to Dahmer's apartment, and is killed.

May 26, 1991 Konerak Sinthasomphone, fourteen, the brother of the boy Dahmer was convicted of molesting, disappears on the day he had soccer practice.

May 27, 1991 Police investigate complaint that a naked, bleeding boy is in the street near the Dahmer apartment. Dahmer persuades police they are homosexual lovers. Dahmer kills Konerak Sinthasomphone.

June 30, 1991 Dahmer meets Matt Turner, twenty, in a Chicago bus station after Gay Pride parade. Turner is killed, his body dismembered and later found in Dahmer's apartment.

July 5, 1991 Dahmer meets Jeremiah Weinberger,

twenty-three, at a bar in Chicago. Two days later, he tells police, he killed and dismembered him.

July 15, 1991 Dahmer is fired from the Ambrosia Chocolate Company for absenteeism, losing a job he had held for six years. The same day he meets Oliver Lacy on the street and takes him to the apartment and kills him.

July 19, 1991 Dahmer meets Joseph Bradehoft, twenty-five, at a bus stop and takes him home and kills him.

July 22, 1991 Dahmer takes Tracy Edwards to his apartment but Edwards escapes and flags down the police, who arrest Dahmer. The remains of at least eleven human bodies are found in the apartment.

July 24, 1991 Glenda Cleveland reveals she, her daughter, and her niece all told police on the night Konerak Sinthasomphone was murdered that he was not an adult.

July 25, 1991 Dahmer is charged with four counts of intentional homicide, the equivalent of murder in Wisconsin. Bail is set at $1 million.

July 26, 1991 Police Chief Philip Arreola suspends, with pay, the three police officers who investigated the May 27 incident at Dahmer's apartment involving Konerak Sinthasomphone.

Aug. 4, 1991 Authorities dig in yard of Dahmer's boyhood home in Bath Township, Ohio, and discover shards of human bones.

Aug. 6, 1991 Dahmer is charged with eight more murders and bail is raised to $5 million. Thief steals $6,000 from grieving family.

Aug. 7, 1991 Milwaukee Police Association, by an overwhelming vote, says it has no confidence in Chief Arreola. Officials ignore it.

Aug. 10, 1991 Konerak Sinthasomphone is cremated following a traditional Buddhist ceremony.

Aug. 22, 1991 Dahmer is charged with three more slayings in Wisconsin, for a total of fifteen. Ohio prosecutor vows to seek a grand jury indictment for the murder of Steven Hicks. District attorney hints that no charge may be brought on seventeenth victim because of missing remains. Dahmer waives his right to a preliminary hearing.

Jan. 13, 1992 Dahmer changes plea from innocent to guilty, but insane.

Jan. 22, 1992 Trial begins in Milwaukee.

Feb. 15, 1992 Dahmer found guilty on all fifteen counts of murder.

Feb. 17, 1992 Dahmer is sentenced to fifteen consecutive terms of life imprisonment.

May 1, 1992 Dahmer is found guilty of murdering Stephen Hicks in Ohio and is given a sixteenth life sentence.

Nov. 28, 1994 Dahmer is found murdered in a prison restroom while serving his 941-year sentence at the Columbia Correctional Institute.

"AN INVALUABLE BOOK FOR ANYONE WHO WANTS
TO UNDERSTAND SERIAL MURDER."

—Joseph Wambaugh

WHOEVER FIGHTS MONSTERS

My Twenty Years Tracking Serial Killers for the FBI

ROBERT K. RESSLER & TOM SHACHTMAN

He coined the phrase "serial killer", he advised Thomas
Harris on *The Silence of the Lambs*, he has gone where no
else has dared to go: inside the minds of the 20th century's
most prolific serial killers. From Charles Manson to
Edmund Kemper, follow former FBI agent Robert K.
Ressler's ingenious trail from the scene of the crime to the
brain of a killer in this fascinating true crime classic.

"THE REAL THING. ABSOLUTELY MESMERIZING."

—Ann Rule, author of *Small Sacrifices*

**AVAILABLE WHEREVER BOOKS ARE SOLD
FROM ST. MARTIN'S PAPERBACKS**